The Imperfect Union

The Imperfect Union

School Consolidation
& Community
Conflict

Alan Peshkin

**The
University of
Chicago
Press**

Chicago &
London

ALAN PESHKIN, professor of comparative
education at the University of Illinois in
Urbana-Champaign, is the author of *Kanuri
School Children* and *Growing Up American.*

The University of Chicago Press, Chicago 60637
The University of Chicago Press, Ltd., London

Library of Congress Cataloging in Publication Data

Peshkin, Alan.
    The imperfect union.

    Bibliography: p.
    Includes index.
    1. Schools—Centralization—Illinois—Case studies.
2. Community and school—Illinois—Case studies.
I. Title.
LB2861.P47   1982   379.1′535   82-16104
ISBN 0-226-66166-0

For Nancy, David, and Julie:
The sine qua non

Contents

Acknowledgments

Even though the citizens of school district "Unit 110" were emotionally involved in their ever-engaging conflict, they were never too busy to be interviewed or to graciously admit my research assistants and me to their meetings. Their cooperation was essential to the success of my study and they gave it unstintingly. I was fortunate to have talented and energetic research assistance from Mike Agone, Mary Beastall, Elaine Stamm, and Marty Thompson; typing assistance from Barbara Franklin, Pat Lewis, Marcia Chicoine, Judy McClughen, and June Chambliss to advance my manuscript through its many drafts; and the drawing skills of Nancy Peshkin.

I feel particularly indebted to the following friends and colleagues (including the anonymous reviewers) who read all or part of these drafts and offered both advice and needed encouragement: Ann Atkin, Eric Bredo, Walter Feinberg, Gordon Hoke, David Housholder, Fred Jaher, Blair Kling, Bob Porter, Tom Sergiovanni, and Nancy Weinberg.

For financial assistance, as well as all-round understanding and support of my research, Dean Mike Atkin and the College of Education must be singled out. As ever, the University of Illinois Research Board provided generous financial aid. I could not do my work without their help. Nor without the help of my wife, Maryann Peshkin, who always belongs in a class by herself.

Prologue

The Problem

I'm going to write an article for the *School Board Journal* about the life of a first-year superintendent. [Pause.] But no one would believe me, or they'd say I was exaggerating. [Pause.] Unless they already knew about Unit 110!
—Burt Hanson, Superintendent of Schools, 1977–79

Killmer is an Illinois village of nine hundred persons. In 1975 Killmer became so distressed at its school board's decision to close its school that it attempted to secede from the consolidated school district (Unit 110) to which it belonged.[1] At stake for Killmer in the board's decision was its community school, a small grade school, located in the heart of the village, containing a kindergarten and grades 1 through 6, housed in an 1895 building. The consolidation-minded school board hoped to resolve its serious financial problems by reducing the number of operating schools. In the course of several elections supporters of the community-school concept came to constitute a majority on the school board, but Killmer still strove to secede from Unit 110. Even when the board voted to open Killmer's closed school, the village continued its efforts to leave the school district.

Killmer's secessionist attempt is the most recent in a series of events that show Unit 110 to be an imperfect educational union of five politically distinct villages. The district was established on the assumption, usually undisputed, that the primary purpose of schools, overriding all others, is the education of children. This assumption was accepted by the Illinois state legislators whose 1945 decision brought numerous Unit 110s into existence. And it was accepted by the educators of that and succeeding generations who endorsed school consolidation. Yet, to the surprise of consolidation's many true believers, angry voices often questioned the veracity and application of this assumption. In Killmer these voices became a roar. Clearly, at any given moment, people find warrant to believe that schools mean more to them than just the education of their children.

Killmerites would not be comforted to learn that school boards in villages, towns, and cities across the nation are voting to close schools. Nor would they be cheered to know that community and neighborhood responses to these closings often sound as if they drew upon a script that was written in Killmer. Neither company in misery nor national notoriety interested village residents: they merely wanted their grade school to reopen and to count on its remaining open.

1

Consolidated School District Unit 110

The Prelude to Conflict

This book is about conflict over schools in village communities. The conflict is of the type in which groups do not "agree about what they want" and "one side wants the other to accept the values, beliefs or way of life it professes and thus makes unacceptable claims upon the other" (Kreisberg 1973: 28). Somewhat prophetically for the villages in question, sociologist Louis Kreisberg added that in such conflicts "the relationship [between contending groups] may be terminated by secession or by converting the other party" (63).

The midwestern countryside might seem an unlikely setting for conflict. Superhighways carry most travelers past the small-town and village oases that stand out among the area's vast grain fields and occasional farmhouses. From these broad concrete masses, speeding passersby see little more than a flash of grain elevator and gas station. From local roads they would possibly see a somnolent, peaceful place, an unlikely setting for a newsworthy story. Impressions of order and stability dominate. Yet the people who inhabit the farms and towns of this horizon-filled countryside all have vested interests, stakes in some status quo or some proposed change. Moreover, they either live in or identify with some particular community whose history and boundaries distinguish them from their neighbors. Since they are socialized to feel they are members of that community, they may mobilize to defend their community's rights; blessed with a territory, they may become territorial in their reaction to perceived transgression. Realization of these facts begins to dispel the illusion of villages as peaceful places.

The schools in the rural setting serve, for the most part, the individual needs of children for economic, academic, and social success, and they serve our national needs for economic and political development. Sandwiched between these individual and national concerns, however, is one that in quiet times we may not even know exists—the concern for community survival.[1] Its educational corollary is the communal function of schooling, which in numerous ways abets community survival. In troubled times, schools may become battlegrounds as people perceive their school's communal function to be jeopardized by local or state policies.

Such was the case in Unit 110 when in the fall of 1975 its school board voted to close the grade schools in Killmer and Tipton as of the following school year. Tipton, in the face of its loss, was passive; Killmer, without a school in town for perhaps the first time since its 1844 log school was erected, fought like hell. Their story reached the media—and me—and I began several years of research on this ill-fated educational union. That research continues to this very moment. I almost hesitate to open my morning newspaper lest I learn of still one more turn of events to explore, one more set of telephone contacts to make, one more round of interviews to conduct, or one more series of meetings to attend. Those activities dominated the research for this book. With the help of four research assistants I collected all available documentary material (newspaper accounts, school records, minutes, and the like), interviewed some 200 persons having past or present associations with Unit 110—school board members, students and educators, parents, and other local residents—and attended meetings.

Heated school issues inspire meetings. They also inspire fatigue and a yearning for that state of complacency thought to be suitable to times when "things are going well." It is taxing to be mobilized, upsetting to depart from comfortable routines. Yet the often weary and bemused residents of Unit 110 have come to expect still one more turn of events as normal. In time I joined them in the expectation that turmoil is normal, sharing their laughter at the latest episode. But after a while I noted that though they laughed they were not amused: they laughed to keep from crying.

For the fact is that closing a school can be a deadly serious event. It is never accepted by all those affected as a simple, routine matter. Despite the abundance in this century of school closings throughout the United States, when it happens to one's own school, the effects are momentous. We never accept something as a matter of course merely because it has occurred in the lives of our neighbors.

At one time we had a great many small school systems in the United States; one-room grade schools and high schools with graduating classes of under twenty students typified schooling in many places. Now their number has declined sharply: in 1932 we had 127,649 separate school districts but in 1980, only 15,709. The decline of the family farm and the increase of urbanization have combined to undermine the need for so many small schools. And the logic of mass society has extended inevitably to education, engulfing our small village and country schools in consolidation, a process which assumes that larger schools are essential for the educational well-being of our children and the fiscal soundness of our school districts. In fact, one proponent of consolidation, typical of most educators, saw the enlargement of schools as so directly linked to good education that he included its outcomes in his definition: a consolidated school, Carter Good wrote, is "an enlarged school formed by uniting small schools . . . for the purpose of providing better school facilities and increasing educational opportunities" (1951: 344). Good's statement includes outcomes because lay persons and professionals alike had long been inclined to see consolidation as a panacea, the salvation of our declining rural society (Henderson and Gomez 1975: passim). I prefer C.O. Fitzwater's nonevaluative statement that consolidation is simply "the merging of two or more attendance areas to form a larger school" (1953: 4). Fitzwater usefully distinguishes consolidation from reorganization, the latter involving the combination of two or more previously independent school systems in one new and larger school system. Consolidation often but not always accompanies reorganization and, however defined, always involves the closing of at least one school.

Following World War II American education lurched and convulsed, reorganized and consolidated. From mixed sentiments of exultation at the promise of educational gain and of pain at the prospects of communal loss, school districts like Illinois's Unit 110 were born. Illinois clearly mandated reorganization in 1945 (see chap. 2), and since then has maintained a financial aid policy that rewards expanding school systems. Testimony to the state's success is the abundance of hyphenated school districts—Mahomet–Seymour, St. Joe—Ogden, Hoopeston–East Lynn—whose names dot local sports pages. This postwar wave of reorganization and consolidation had its detractors, but their voices were like whispers in the wind. Unwilling to relinquish the past, diehard supporters occasionally maintained the legal status of one-room schools that had no students, and they held on to school systems with only eight, ten, or eleven grades. Notwithstanding these often determined efforts, the closing of beloved schools and the organization of relatively large new school districts occurred in ebullient times, when lay persons and officials alike were cheered by the dream of modern schools leading to grand futures.

Today, on the contrary, it is the twin demons of inflation and plummeting enrollments that compel school districts to consider consolidation or, much less often, reorganization, in times unbrightened by promises of betterment. Nonetheless, school closing emerges everywhere as the most usual solution to the financial and demographic problems that plague schools. Unlike the consolidations of the postwar era, present efforts are not directed mainly at remote, underpopulated rural counties with a plethora of tiny schools. Unit 110 joins both larger and smaller systems in the need to find solutions to genuinely urgent financial problems.

The search for solutions may be confounded by an uneasy relationship among the villages that originally united to form a new school district. At their simplest, consolidated school districts combine two previously separate villages and their school systems, usually one that is small and another that is big enough and active enough to provide compelling arguments (and votes) for decisions about which schools to keep open, where to locate new buildings, what to include in the curriculum, and the like. At their most complex, they unite several school systems, and the involved towns are vocal, intact, and wary of merger from the outset—reluctant brides, so to speak. Indeed, educational unions are like marriages: some begin uncertainly but grow in trust and confidence as time heals the wounds of their stressful, externally inspired mergers; for others the mistrust and uncertainty remain indefinitely, their linkages thin and the partners quick to anger, turning backward for solace to golden, prereorganization days. Unit 110's merger is one of the latter type. Its thirty-year history testifies to the range of problems that may result from linking villages where differences of perception and values prevail.

One set of perceptions and values led Unit 110's school board to close schools; another set prompted Killmer residents' enraged reactions. Other Unit 110 residents were upset, but largely because Killmer's behavior disrupted school district routines. These other residents long wondered what the issues could possibly be that would so inflame Killmerites. Eventually, many began to understand. Meanwhile, name calling, threats, and rumors abounded. "Board members Parke and Clore sold us out. They think only of their own towns and schools." "We never should have come together in the first place. We didn't get along in the past and we don't get along now." "Killmer has always wanted its own way. They always think me first—what's good for *me!*" "It all goes back to the beginning and it'll never end."

"It," of course, refers to the turmoil in the school district. The observation is on the mark in directing one back to the

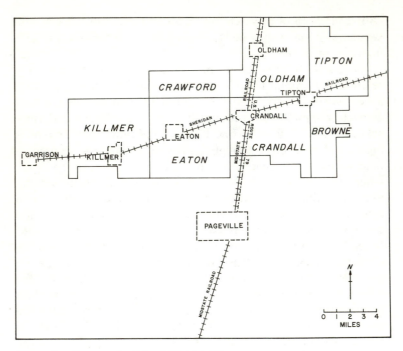

Figure 1.   Community School District 110

beginning of Unit 110 if one is to understand the present disorder. And, unhappily, it may not be wrong in suggesting, too,
that "it'll never end."

The Setting of the Conflict

Village Facts

    West of the Appalachian Mountains human settlements
often arose adjacent to railroad lines. Little nubs of people may
have existed in an area before a rail line was built, but a firm
basis for development awaited the railroad. This is the background of Unit 110's villages, each of which is located on a
rail line (see fig. 1). Killmer, Eaton, Crandall, and Tipton are
on a southwest-northeast axis formed by the Sheridan line,
while Oldham and Crandall are on a north-south axis formed

by the Midstate line. Crandall is clearly the central village; it stands at the intersection of these two rail lines and is located on the highway that leads to Pageville, a city of seventy-five thousand, the county seat and major source of local employment. Crandall's strategic location made it the largest of the five villages and, in strictly logical terms, the prime location for any centrally located school building which would serve the entire Unit 110 district. Situated together west of Pageville Road, Killmer and Eaton are neighbors and allies in school strife; they became known as the "West Side." But as will become clear, it is their ideology rather than their geography that joins them so firmly. Crandall, Oldham, and Tipton are known as the "East Side," although they do not plan or consciously side together.

How far away must one be from a point to feel on the edge of the space that encompasses that point? Unit 110's 173 square miles constitute the school district's space; Crandall, as noted, is its central geographic point, whereas Killmer, thirteen miles from Crandall, feels it is located on its edge. Of the five villages, Killmer is in fact the farthest from Crandall; Eaton and Tipton are eight and Oldham is five miles from Crandall. Moreover, located at the district's western periphery, Killmer is only five miles from the village of Garrison, site of the Garrison Unit School District. Killmer's proximity to Garrison eventually became a factor in the conflict spawned by the 1975 school-closing decision. If, in Unit 110, there is a sense of being peripheral or central, it applies essentially to school affairs. The distance measured in round-trip time spent carting children to and from school events is annoying and costly. The distance reflected in distress over decisions which closed schools and caused children to be bused to Crandall is unbearable, a call to arms.

If distance contains both a quantitative and a qualitative or psychological dimension, so does population size. Villagers can discriminate one place from another which in terms of appearance do not seem strikingly dissimilar. Crandall, with two thousand people, is twice the size of the next largest village. Is a village of two thousand rightfully accused of urban ways? Yes, if you can accept the impressions of Unit 110 residents who, contrary to the facts, see Crandall as a hotbed of immorality engendered by a population of transient, trailer camp, and divorced persons.

Before continuing, I must dispose of a small detail of little importance here, but one that could cause confusion later. Up to this point I have referred only to Unit 110's five villages, not to its townships. Each village is located within a township of the same name, part or all of which is included in the school district. In addition to these five townships, Unit 110 contains parts of two small (population under two hundred), village-less townships—Crawford and Browne—which enter the chronicle as participants in the so-called gentleman's agreement discussed later. Throughout what follows, when the townships are referred to, it is those parts of the townships lying within Unit 110 that are meant, and sometimes more especially their rural areas in distinction to the villages.

The school-district population embraces both the village and the rural residents of each township. During the half-century preceding 1970 the rural population, with one exception, has declined; the one exception is Crandall, whose countryside reaches southward toward Pageville. Contrary to what has happened in the county's villages, job opportunities in Pageville have expanded since 1950. Villages close to Pageville grew in population as newcomers combined urban jobs with village or rural living. Eaton grew the most in terms of percentage from 1950 to 1970, Crandall the most in actual numbers. The fifty-year population statistics for Unit 110 shown in table 1 (all tables appear in the Appendix) epitomize the twentieth-century demography of rural America.

In addition to size, a number of other attributes vary from township to township and provide a basis for comparison. All school-district residents are Caucasians; the only possible exceptions are six persons in Crandall noted as "other." Over 75 percent of the people in each township are Illinois natives; the range is from 76.8 percent in Crandall to 91.3 percent in Tipton. The following personal data are taken from the 1970 census. See table 2 for a summary of some of these figures.

Education. Except for Killmer's low of 55.4 percent, about 62 percent of the persons in the five townships constituting most of Unit 110 attended or completed high school. Persons in Crandall and Eaton have the highest probability of completing high school; persons in Killmer have the lowest probability.

College attendance rates vary widely, ranging from Crandall's and Eaton's highs of 21 and 19.1 percent, respectively, to Killmer's 15.9 percent and Tipton's low of 10.9 percent. Of all those who attend college, about 50 percent graduate, except in Tipton, where the figure is 39.7 percent. Tipton has no residents with graduate degrees, but in the other four townships the percentage varies from Oldham's low of 2.4 to Crandall's high of 7.2 percent; Killmer occupies the middle of the group with 4.1 percent. In Crandall, 315 persons received post–high school education; the rest of the district together has 417 such persons.

Marital status. Eaton has the highest percentage (2.3) of divorced persons. Killmer is next with 1.8 percent, followed by Crandall with 1.5 percent. If we group divorced persons with those whose marriages are disrupted in some way (spouse absent or separated), then such persons contribute about the same proportion—2.2 or 2.3 percent— of persons aged fourteen or older in four of the townships. Tipton is lowest at 1.9 percent.

Family income. Except for Killmer, the median-range income for all townships is $10,000–$11,999; for Killmer it is $8,000–$8,999. Killmer has the most families (21.2 percent) earning under $5,000; Eaton has the fewest (9.6 percent), followed by Crandall (12.3 percent), Oldham (13.2 percent), and Tipton (17.9 percent).

With 135 persons listed at below poverty level (based on the federal government's 1970 definition as a family of four having an annual income under $3,721), Killmer ranks highest in absolute numbers and, at 9.1 percent, also has the highest proportion, followed by Oldham (7.3 percent), Tipton (3.9 percent), Eaton (3.6 percent), and Crandall (3.2 percent).

Occupations. As indicated by the percentages of persons reporting themselves farmers or farm managers, Oldham (15.5 percent) and Killmer (13.1) are the most agriculturally oriented townships. Crandall, at 3.5 percent, is the least. Crandall also has the highest percentage of professionals (22.4) and the lowest percentage of low-skilled workers (17.6). Killmer has the lowest percentage of professionals (13.7), close to Oldham's 14.7 percent; Tipton has the highest percentage of low-skilled workers (27.6), followed by Oldham (24.3), Eaton (23.6), and Killmer (21.5).

Although Killmer and Eaton clearly differ in educational, financial, and occupational terms, they stand together on the single question that has most aroused them since the origin of Unit 110: the retention of complete kindergarten-through-eighth-grade (K–8) schools in their own communities.

Village impressions. Census data permit the creation of a useful picture of a place, one that allows ready comparisons and contrasts. What such data do not reveal is the sense that the residents of such a place have about themselves and about their relationship with other places, a sense that is derived from a compound of historical and contemporary fact and fiction. There is virtually no locale so small that it lacks a history distinguishing it from other locales that seem to look just like it. Its distinctiveness (no matter if it exists only in the eyes of the residents) sets it apart from others, makes it conscious of and sensitive to its boundaries, and gives rise to a feeling of inside-outside and of we-they. Listen, for example, to how Unit 110 residents view themselves and others.

Chuck Schultz, a farmer and native of Oldham, thinks the villages are different. "Each has got different morality," he says. "Been there all the time," though he can't elaborate beyond noting that Crandall is Methodist, Presbyterian, and non-Catholic; Tipton is Lutheran; and Eaton and Oldham are Catholic. The latter three villages had parochial grade schools; Eaton still does. Schultz believes "parochial kids are more dignified and respectful of authority than the nonparochial kids of Killmer and Crandall." He adds, without connecting his thoughts, "there was something about Killmer [that] people didn't like."

Speaking with the vehemence common to the politically mobilized Killmerite, Robbie Miller, native and farmer, contrasts Crandall and all other villages in Unit 110 in terms that one hears often in Killmer:

> Historically there's differences between these towns. We quit playing Crandall in basketball my freshman year. Last game there was almost a drag-out fight. Now us and Eaton has been real rivals, with lot of friction whenever we play. Still we always parted as friends. Never had any trouble with Tipton or Oldham. Crandall was noted as dirty players.

Miller concludes with a sentiment that he is not pleased to hold; it is one that is central to understanding the chronicle of Unit 110. He utters it slowly, regretfully:

> You change generations, but I guess you don't change the thought, the basic thought in the home. We remember. You forget the score, but you don't forget how the game was played. I try not to let that influence my thinking. Still there is some bitterness toward Crandall from the start.

Miller and Ray Reinhart, Killmer native and merchant, have been battling school boards on behalf of Killmer for years. They have schemed and argued and organized, generally reaching the same conclusions, though not by the same route. Reinhart does not discount the legacy of bitterness between Killmer and Crandall generated by athletic rivalry; he focuses, rather, on Crandall's current attributes—it has "more of a larger city image" and is more of a bedroom town. "It's not so much who works outside the community," says Reinhart, "as how much interest they take. The people who don't get involved—don't really care about what happens—those are your real bedroom people." What is unquestionably true is that Killmer and Eaton each has its own bank and stores that are open and available for shopping; Oldham and Tipton do not. Thus, reasons Reinhart, people from those towns have to shop and bank in nearby

Crandall and "the effect of driving out of town is the feeling that since we have to go to Crandall anyway, why not have our school there."

Lenore Ames, Killmer native, ticks off her points about the villages:

> Oldham and Tipton are easier going; they don't get uptight so quickly. Crandall, it's cliquish there, so if you're not with the in crowd, you don't get the time of day. People there just don't seem to care. They've got more retirees, older people, transients, people in new, low-rent apartments, trailer-court people, and people who don't stay around too long or vote. They know they're not going to lose their school [the high school and junior high] because no other village has a suitable building. Eaton is just like Killmer. Not much difference living in either place.

Among residents of the five villages, there's almost a consensus about Crandall. Despite having a population of only about two thousand persons, it is accused of having "picked up the ways of a larger city. People are transient, not so close, so neighborly." Indeed, even Crandall residents present a negative view of their village. Marty Finder, retired Crandall native:

> People move here because it's cheaper to live and also because of the racial problem in Pageville. We had only eight or nine people at the last village caucus. It was pitiful.

John Gilbert, Crandall merchant and resident: "If you want to get involved here you've got to put your foot forward; not too many people do."

In general, Oldham and Tipton do not elicit reactions as sharp, explicit, or negative as those aimed at their sister communities. They are the smallest villages; the voice of protest is little heard from them. Both have dead business sections, their residents now fully dependent on outside places except for gas, alcohol, and religion. Oldham resident Chuck Schultz:

> Oldham's changed. It's dying. Used to have banks, grocery stores, a hardware, blacksmith. We've got more people

than ever before, but I think when they put in a good road to Pageville in 1924, cars came, and that killed the town.

Eaton resident Peggy Harwood:

Oldham always has a core group who get involved. They're for a centralized junior high, think the West Side is crazy and selfish, and don't want to put money into old buildings. I have friends there and we don't even talk school. We'd just get in a fight.

Oldham resident Ed Kling:

We have a village board, but they're not prestigious. Status is not a big thing in town. Some have more money than others, but they don't have any weight. In terms of the school, I don't think anyone can influence anyone else.

Similar comments are in fact heard about each town except Eaton—that there's no power structure, no prestigious person who carries weight in town. A Killmerite, possibly reflecting her distress at the years of stubborn educational issues, wished there was someone who could quietly run things, as the banker Thomas Stoughton of Crandall used to. "If Thomas was pro-something, then that got across because Thomas could get out the vote." Mostly, however, Crandall is labeled "the sleeping giant," because while its population is large enough to swing any election, its political apathy has led consistently to defeats at the hand of Eaton and Killmer voting as a bloc.

Killmer and Eaton, the West Side allies in years of educational controversy, share the sentiment that they truly are communities, places where people care. They are perceived as different, however, in important ways. Peggy Harwood, the Eaton native quoted above on the subject of Oldham (and whose neighbor is a Unit 110 teacher), depicts the differences:

The Killmer kids are [academically] behind the Eaton kids, probably because they never had a strong administrator at Killmer. Eaton has always had a stable staff. Killmer kids always have first-year teachers. In general, there's a lower caliber of kids in Killmer's homes; there's much more van-

dalism there. Probably more broken homes. Six of the kids
from Killmer my friend has are always in trouble.

Harwood's comments reflect the situation in the school year
1976–77, when Killmer Grade School was closed and its students spent the year in Eaton.

Finally, the Hudsons display an affectionately critical view
of Killmer, their adopted home. They love living in Killmer
and believe it contains "some of the finest people in the world,"
as well as chronic fighters and agitators. "If you give Killmerites exactly what they want," Mr. Hudson observes,
"they'll find something wrong. If the good Lord would plan
things, they still wouldn't be happy."

School district facts. Unit 110's complex social reality provides the occasion for setting forth a range of data. But just
as this book's particular story and its interpretation represent
a selection from among several possible stories and interpretations, so do the facts noted here represent a selection. They
relate mostly to the changing number of students in the school
district from kindergarten through grade 12; to the changing
location of these students in the various school buildings of the
five villages; and to the school district's changing financial
picture.

Unit 110 opened its doors as a new school district in 1948.
The enrollment picture in its constituent school systems in the
years preceding its establishment, especially at the high school
level, illustrates the major reason for Illinois's encouraging the
establishment of larger school districts throughout the state.
In 1947, for example, the total enrollment in grades 9 to 12 was
18 in Oldham, 59 in Eaton, 62 in Killmer, 68 in Tipton, and 90
in Crandall (see table 3). Together, of course, the five systems
could form a high school of reasonable size, with 297 students,
and it was clearly the association of size and enhanced high
school opportunities that inspired the formation of Unit 110;
the district's residents and founders contemplated no major
changes in the grade schools of the five systems.

Like most school systems in the United States, Unit 110
experienced an enrollment boom and bust. It grew not only as

a result of the postwar baby boom but also because of its proximity to Pageville, a city with many job opportunities. And also like most school systems, Unit 110 eventually declined in numbers of students and employees and in financial resources (see table 4). School records are missing for the period 1949–61, but those available for 1962–78 establish the quantitative basis for the school issues that dominate this study. They are, simply, that from 1962 to 1969 the number of students and the number of school employees increased with no corresponding increase in space. After 1969, both student enrollment and state aid declined. Notwithstanding these declines, the number of employees continued to increase until 1975, the year in which Unit 110's school board, at the urging of the superintendent, instituted cutbacks and voted to close schools in Killmer and Tipton. Financial receipts generally kept pace with expenditures until 1970; after 1970 they generally did not (see table 5).

Despite the community school's appeal and its place in American educational tradition, Unit 110 could not uphold this tradition. While Crandall outgrew its own building, Tipton and Oldham had classroom space to spare; in addition, some buildings were old, and disrepair hampered their utility. The net result, shown in table 6, is a shifting pattern, notably for Crandall and Tipton children, who moved now here and now there with a frequency that must belie anyone's conception of rationality; ever tenacious about their community school, and with the enrollment and space to support their commitment, Killmer and Eaton children moved much less frequently. Oldham children enjoyed the greatest stability of all, but this was largely the result of their fortuitous location and comparatively sound building rather than of commitment to their community school.

In their own way, the shifting organizational patterns tell the story of Unit 110. Behind these patterns is the story of what was happening to the children of the district as their parents and educators agitated over varying conceptions not of what or how children should be taught but of where they should attend school. For some parents the where not only contributed to but overwhelmed the what; for others the what completely encompassed their concerns. "Get on with educating the kids," the latter group asserted, their increasing exasperation and impatience directed toward those who seemed always to talk "communities and not kids." "Close our school and you'll kill our town" was the former's succinct reply.

The Imperfect Union

This book is meant to be a thick slice of educational life, replete with details that otherwise might be unavailable to future students of education. A slice of life by its very name promises to deliver a complete picture of some segment of reality. Of course, I fail to keep this promise. Judgments are made and selections result. I cannot recover all the events of the past, and I give priority to some persons and perspectives and not to others. The result is a partial and (I hope) not too arbitrary rendering of a troubled period in the educational and community life of Unit 110 residents. In the interest of emphasizing the most important issues and of achieving some brevity and readability, I have often delimited events so as to get on with the recounting of Unit 110's past and present troubles.

Selection is not an objective act; it cannot be. By the time I came to write this book, I had lived for a long time with my story—that is, the one I saw in the data I collected. Nevertheless, I have meant to provide a basis for understanding the varied aspects of the calamity that befell Unit 110 and its constituent villages. I have not tried to capitalize fully on the opportunity to interpret all these aspects, to draw out their multiple implications. What was important for me was to tell the story that seemed most worth telling and then to explore what it means in human terms.

At one level, this book relates the story of Unit 110, its decision to close Killmer's school, and how and why Killmer so strenuously resisted this decision. At another level, it illuminates issues that transcend the particulars of Unit 110. These issues include (1) the nature of communities and their boundaries; (2) the nature of the school union that is created when several previously separate school districts are consolidated into a single district; (3) the behavior of communities in conflict over school affairs; and, most important, (4) the meaning of a school to a community.

After my research assistants and I had established ourselves as fixtures at school-board meetings, citizens' advisory committee meetings, concerned citizens' meetings, and the like, I became party to a common exchange: "When you going to write your book?" I'd be asked. I'd answer, "When nothing's happening and we can stop going to meetings." Eventually I decided that any stopping point would be arbitrary and that I had learned enough to portray Unit 110's educational union, fated, so it seems, to living under a Chinese curse. The Chinese are said to damn their enemies to conducting their lives in interesting times. What a curious condemnation! Usually equating interesting with good, we label movies, people, or artistic performances as "interesting." But when interesting is an abiding, persistent attribute of the times, the quality assumes a different aspect, one less pleasing than that provided by the superior performance or the well-crafted movie. "Interesting times" seems to refer to periods astir with newsworthy events that disrupt our lives, and not to a pleasing transitory occasion like a holiday at the seashore. As a result of the disruption of such times, the security and certainty we seem to seek and need elude us. It is one village's response to these concerns of security and certainty which constitutes the central focus of this book.

2

The Troubled Early Years: 1945–62

It is fair to say: That the school which serves its community best is the school which best serves its state and nation.
—Merle Sumption and Yvonne Engstrom, *School Community Relations*

Schools are organized primarily for the benefit of the children who attend them, and not for the benefit of the adults who control them. . . . Reorganization may simply require shift of allegiance to a larger school.
—*Pageville Press*, November 4, 1947

The Crusade for Reorganization: Unit 110 is Born

In June 1945, the sixty-fourth General Assembly of the State of Illinois passed that year's House Bill 406. It was one month after Germany had signed an unconditional surrender and three months before Japan did the same. The war had placed a moratorium on attempts to "modernize" education, but with the war as good as won, the legislature passed "An Act in relation to the survey and re-organization of school districts and making an appropriation therefore" (*Manual for County School Survey Committees* 1945: 39). By this act Illinois meant to expedite the development of larger school systems and thereby to close down those little centers of nostalgia which then abounded in rural America—the one-room school.

Nostalgia counted for little as the case emerged for larger school systems. Farm groups, urban-based professors, educational associations, and politicians were impressed by these facts: in 1940, 3.5 million school-aged rural youth were not enrolled in school; in 1945–46, rural children were in school 167 days, compared with 181 days for urban children; in 1942, annual per-pupil expenditure was $86 for rural students compared with $124 for urban students; also in 1942, the rural teacher's annual salary averaged $967, as against the urban teacher's earnings of $1,937 (cost-of-living differentials were not identified) (Sumption and Beem 1947: 10–12). If such data suffice to characterize rural schooling, then, indeed, the rural student was relatively deprived. In any event, remedies for these shortcomings were not sought within rural school systems as they were constituted. "Reorganization" was mandated. No organized group of any prominence resisted the allure its educational changes promised to children and parents long accustomed to outhouses and hand-operated pumps even, the enthusiasts asserted, in the midst of the richest farmland in the entire country.

Enter House Bill 406 and its requirement that Illinois county officials must meet with all their local school board members by December 15, 1945, and decide by vote whether to organize a nine-member school survey committee. If the majority agreed, then a county's school board members would separate into two groups, one from the urban and one from the rural areas, with the former electing four representatives and the latter five. No one appeared to protest this gerrymandered arrangement. In the course of its deliberations, the committee was abetted by professors who jumped on the bandwagon of reorganization. Merle Sumption, then of the University of Illinois, was one of many who articulated this newly generated thrust in American education. Reorganization, Sumption (and coauthor Beem) clarified, must be distinguished from consolidation: reorganization refers "to the alteration of administrative districts," whereas consolidation refers "to the merging of attendance areas or schools" (6) within an administrative district. The former was the charge of the county survey committees and the latter, if it occurred, would be the decision of the new school boards that were to be formed following reorganization. For example, reorganization can be said to have occurred when the forty-two separate elementary districts and the five separate high school districts merged to form the new administrative entity that became known as Unit 110. The seven-person school board that House

Bill 406 provided to run these new unit districts would have to determine which of Unit 110's then forty-seven attendance areas would be consolidated—in the name of reasonableness, efficiency, and economy—and thereby disappear. Sumption supported the state's reorganization campaign with a presentation of the reorganizer's argument that the new, larger schools would bring about better education because of their increased capacity to provide libraries, laboratories, supplies, and equipment. If there were doubters of this claim, few if any persons could make a tenable case for Page County's more than two hundred independent rural school districts.

Editor Glenn Davids of the *Killmer News* perhaps came as close to so arguing as anyone in Page County. He alone of all the doubters had a front-page weekly arena for hurling his barbs against those so-called modernizers who saw virtue both in the closing of local schools and in the dilution of local control that followed reorganization. When he retired in 1952, he had spent forty vocal years at the helm of the *Killmer News,* effortlessly assuming the role of Killmer's conscience, as so many old-time country editors did for their communities.[1]

In the 1940s, it took little persuasion to enlist persons from all social classes in the chorus of praise for expanded school systems. Nonetheless, Davids's gloomy forecasts reached a local constituency that joined him in lamenting the merging of two nearby high school districts. The time was April 1946, in the midst of the school survey committee's work, but some high school districts already had begun to consider reorganization. Such action would be unwise for Killmer, Davids declared, because it would "cause our property to decrease in value and we would soon be on a fair road to becoming another desolation like some other villages which once were thriving towns." Davids's wail of communal woe and Sumption's vision of scholastic euphoria were the poles between which sentiment in Unit 110 would flow.

The school survey committee's official deliberations were conducted in secrecy. Not until November 1, 1947, when it planned to disseminate a *Tentative Report,* would the public learn which of several plans the committee actually preferred.

Throughout 1946 and 1947 the probable alternative plans became the subject of formal discussion among all affected communities. Would Page County become one, two, three, seven, or eight school districts, as different groups proposed? Professors from Pageville College took to the radio to rail against "small, inadequate school districts" and to argue the case for schools which "meet the needs of people living in this modern world." They held three-day conferences and pledged their resources "for a concentrated attack upon the problems involved in reorganization." And they attended public meetings in Killmer and Eaton and Crandall to advocate what Davids called their "super school district" plan consisting of one large high school and five to six grade schools for the entire northern half of Page County. Should this happen, Davids warned, Killmer students would have no chance for a successful future. Therefore he proposed a merger of Killmer with Eaton: together they would be large enough to justify maintaining their own high school. This proposed linkage of Killmer and Eaton reversed his view of such mergers enunciated one year earlier, and foreshadowed their future conjoint action on many subsequent occasions.

Agitation mounted in the month before the committee's report was due to be released. Representatives from thirty-two different women's groups met in Pageville to discuss reorganization. They complained of public apathy toward the nine-member survey group and its two-year study, urged the survey group to create a single school district for the entire county, and criticized the county superintendent for his endorsement of an eight-district plan. Rural persons reacted to the possibility of a one-district plan by rejecting any plan that united them with the city of Pageville; they were unmoved by the argument that only a single, countywide district would give all the county's children equal educational opportunity. The League of Women Voters sponsored talks by Pageville College professors, one of whom proclaimed that all educators would agree that a one-district plan is best, a three-district plan next best, and that the absolute minimum size for a high school is three hundred students.

Within days of these talks, the school survey committee's *Tentative Report* announced its eight-district plan to replace Page County's existing 223 districts. Of the five villages that eventually became Unit 110, Crandall, Oldham, and Tipton (plus a fourth village) formed one of these eight districts, while Killmer and Eaton (plus three more villages) formed another.

The agitation that built up during the months the committee had deliberated now had a concrete target—the *Tentative Report*. It contained many recommendations (such as a uniform tax rate in each district; "special guidance in music, art, and physical education"; special facilities for physically and mentally handicapped children; and a coordinated transportation system), but these were virtually ignored in the northern third of Page County, where Unit 110's villages were located, because there the central issue was which villages and townships in fact would join with which other villages and townships in the new districts to be formed. The voice of the people, as yet unheard, would be given its chance in spring 1948, when the electorate of each existing school district would vote. It was clear, however, from the time the *Tentative Report* was released, that neither Killmer and Eaton nor Crandall, Oldham, and Tipton were happy with their suggested districts.

Glenn Davids stated unequivocally that no one in Killmer and Eaton favored the eight-district plan. Pageville College professors labeled the *Tentative Report* "inferior" because it "does not provide large enough districts to support economically a broad educational program, violates community boundaries, or both." Lawyer Simon Garrot of Crandall, an educational activist, mobilized public opinion through open meetings and through personal contact with other community leaders. In the period before the *Tentative Report* was published, he chaired a group of north Page County people who hoped to organize a school district large enough for a "broader curriculum, and more modern facilities and administration than are possible in small schools." "Modern" was an important attribute to Garrot. He, too, felt that the eight-district plan violated community boundaries. He sought a school district that could offer "equal educational opportunities to all"; this phrase would become a watchword in Unit 110 for persons of opposing points of view. Citizens in the Unit 110 area were subjected to the pressure and persuasion of petitions and meetings. Garrot assured them that his reorganization plan, which would join all five of the villages already mentioned in one school district, would honor the existing village schools, maintaining an "attendance unit of eight grades, and possibly nine, in each town." (Thirty years later, school-district residents would recall this stipulation as an inviolable part of what became known as the "gentleman's agreement," a set of understandings meant to direct Unit 110 policy and practice.) They were also told that it would be necessary, eventually, to build a centrally located high school.

The vote on April 10, 1948, was a victory for Garrot and company, but only by a hair. Davids bannered his front page with the news, "Vote Community School Unit by One Majority"; a Pageville paper cut this figure by 50 percent—"Number 110 Okayed by Half Vote." The vote was affirmative, however one tallied the ballots, but the voting pattern deserves further elaboration for the light it sheds on voter sentiment. To pass, the proposal had to win majority approval in two separate referenda, one held in the villages and the other in the rural precincts. The rural voters approved the proposal by a very slim margin; years later farmers would speculate that had they voted rather than farmed that April day in 1948, there would be no Unit 110 today. In the villages, the overall results were substantially positive, but note the distribution shown in table 7.

Oldham did not assert strong views about any aspect of the reorganization during the years of the school survey committee's work. Of all five villages, Oldham alone was convinced it did not possess a viable high school; for the period 1944–48, it never had more than eighteen pupils in its entire four-year high school. Thus Oldham had the least to lose by joining a large school district. Crandall's overwhelming affirmative vote confirmed Garrot's talent as publicist, and Eaton left no doubt of its support for the same point of view. Killmer, on the contrary, in its one-vote approval of Unit 110, demonstrated the ambivalence which would persistently underlie its response to

Unit 110. Tipton solidly rejected the plan for Unit 110, as it would reject most plans of any sort in subsequent years.

As of July 1, 1948, all the old school boards were dissolved and replaced by a single school board. Before this happened, however, a large group of existing board members, educators, and citizens met in Crandall to clarify procedures for selecting the new Unit 110 board members. The results were incorporated in a gentleman's agreement stipulating that on the eve of a board election each of the seven townships in Unit 110 would hold a caucus to choose a candidate; each township would support its own candidate; and only caucus-endorsed candidates would be supported by the other townships. While it was perfectly legal for non-caucus-endorsed candidates to seek election, district sentiment strongly favored always having one person from each township on the school board. Davids liked this gentlemen's agreement because it calmed his fear that reorganization might disenfranchise his village. Neither Davids nor any other observer pointed out that when the agreement promised a representative from each township, it reinforced the idea that a board member should represent township rather than unitwide interests and thereby encouraged a parochialism that ever after would haunt Unit 110.

House Bill 406, passed before World War II was over, clearly achieved its purpose of reducing the number of school districts in Illinois. Unit 110 was one offspring of this legislation. Perhaps it was appropriate that Page County's school survey committee concluded its June 1948 *Final Report* with words that reflected the innocent hopes of postwar America:

> Science won the war. America can hope to be strong and safe if we give our citizens a much better education. It is through better education that we can produce a united, peaceful world. States must exercise their responsibility to make school districts satisfactory channels for good education as well as good instruments of local control. School district reorganization is a key to better education, and an improved education holds the key to a safer, better world. Think constructively and act wisely.

An educational birth had occurred and the infant school district, its legs awobble, prepared to face its hosts and their children—though in this account it is the behavior of the hosts that commands our attention.

June–December 1948: The Shape of the Future

More ended in June 1948 than just another school year; this month marked the demise of the forty-seven separate school districts which together constituted Unit 110. The new superintendent took over at the end of June; corn and soybean fields had been planted weeks earlier; and Page County had begun to adjust to its characteristically deep, moist summer heat when Editor Davids struck his warning bell.

Davids had scant time to enjoy the new school board's decisions to keep Killmer's grade school and high school open for the 1948–49 school year and to purchase two buses for the rural Killmer children, because the board soon began to contemplate the future of Unit 110. For Davids and others who loved the past, contemplating the future meant exploring opportunities for change, and change spelled danger to the things of the past. Hindsight suggests that the board should have postponed any but its most urgent plans in order to give Unit 110 residents time to adjust to the dramatic changes that had just occurred in the educational aspect of their lives. It did not, and the results of the school board's contemplation, contained in its September 8 resolution, distressed Davids.

The resolution reasoned that because small schools are an obstacle to educational progress, the board should appoint ''a committee of at least three qualified, unbiased persons'' to conduct a survey and make suitable recommendations. This committee was invited to consider:

> Should we attempt in some way to enlarge our high school attendance units by the opening of school in the fall of 1949? Are there buildings in the system that are adequate

for consolidating the number of pupils that are in the upper four years of high school?

The implications of this memorandum must be articulated. A mere two weeks after the newly formed school district opened its doors for the first time, its school board empowered a committee to explore the enlargement of "our high school attendance units." This could only mean the closing of Killmer High School and the transport of its students to the one high school large enough to contain all the district's secondary students—Crandall's. If, at this time, one's eye is not on the gleam of those academic plums promised by larger educational facilities, then one faces the prospect of adding a new loss—the village high school—to a still unassimilated old one—local control of one's village schools. In short, if one is enthralled by the "gains" of reorganization, then one is not troubled by their "costs"; but, of course, the converse also is true.

The three "qualified" persons who agreed to serve on Unit 110's future-looking committee reviewed the unit's academic program, but attended mostly to its buildings. They pronounced Crandall's, Oldham's, and Tipton's buildings "sound" and Killmer's and Eaton's "unsound." Killmer's building was suitable for a few more years "before it will be absolutely necessary to construct a new building." Eaton's was condemned as "an old building which should not be used longer than is absolutely necessary." The committee advised: (1) a 6-3-3 plan of one six-grade elementary school in each of the five villages; two three-year junior high schools, one in Killmer and one in Tipton; and one three-year senior high school at Crandall. (This plan was implemented in 1949 and remained in effect until 1953. Many years later, Unit 110 school board member Harry Walter would recall this period with anger unmoderated by the passage of time. Walter was a student in Eaton High School in 1948. With only his senior year left, Eaton High was closed and he had to complete his schooling in Crandall. He felt betrayed then and he still does.) And (2) the employment of additional personnel, including a full-time assistant to the superintendent, a guidance director, a school nurse, a school librarian, three music teachers, and a speech-correction or a remedial-reading specialist. Clearly, this three-man committee operated in the spirit of reorganization's promise; it sought those changes that size would make possible. In 1948 most Americans accepted this outlook as conventional wisdom.

Glenn Davids was one of the exceptions:

> There has been a storm of protests . . . concerning the recommendations made last week to operate only one high school in Unit 110 next year. The three educators who made the survey probably meant well—but too often they see only the educational viewpoint. Do you realize what this plan would mean to Killmer Township?

Perhaps the plan's implications were self-evident to readers of the *News* because Davids elaborated only two points: (1) Some students would have to travel thirty-two miles round trip each day to Crandall High School, when a school in Garrison was only a ten-mile round trip away. (2) An addition to Crandall High School would have to be built because he believed it could not accommodate all eligible children, and "everyone," Davids observed, "realizes today the cost of building is prohibitive." Davids's motives seem to be avoiding long bus travel and increased educational costs. Whatever the case, Davids could not be accused of seeing reorganization from an educational viewpoint.

Eatonites also rejected the committee's short-term plan to consolidate the district's high school. Better to retain all existing high schools, their spokesmen advocated, than set a precedent for locating the proposed master high school in Crandall, instead of in the country, where it belongs. Their motive seems to have been to avoid creating a de facto situation that would benefit Crandall more than Eaton and the other villages. Crandall, with nothing to lose, could not oppose the unitwide use of its high school; Oldham, close to Crandall and with almost no high school enrollment of its own, supported the plan; and Tipton, with its own high school in jeopardy, was curiously unmoved one way or the other. While Tipton residents would seldom fail to register their negativism when it came time to vote, they were virtually mute on those occasions when voicing distress might have led to outcomes they favored.

On December 9, 1948, the board took action on the committee's proposals and by a 5-2 vote agreed to establish a three-year high school in Crandall. The school board acknowledged the opposition to its decision, but hoped people would understand that its intent was a better school system.

Davids headlined his reaction to the board's vote, "Board Votes One High School for Unit 110." Building upon the comments of Killmer and Eaton board members that their constituents opposed a single, districtwide high school, Davids made a gloomy forecast: "The fate of Unit 110 hangs in the balance. . . . Many take the view that since the 'east' voted solidly against the 'west,' they [Killmer and Eaton] can read between the lines as to what will happen when an election is held to build a new school building." Of course, reasons Davids, since the West Side controls a minority of the votes, the new school will be built *in* Crandall. Thus, Eaton would be better off merging with Pageville, and Killmer should look to Garrison: "If Garrison and Garrison Township will vote favorably to form a district, Killmer will petition out of Unit 110 and join that district. This is where Killmer Township should be. We have merely attempted to give the facts in this matter. . . ." Before Unit 110's first semester was complete, it heard the rumblings of secession.[2]

The Secession Issue (1949–51)

Editor Davids stirred up local discontent over the consolidation of the four, pre–Unit 110 high schools into one high school building located in Crandall. The school board endeavored to soften this discontent by encouraging citizen initiative to identify a suitable site for a new, master high school. By the end of March 1949 citizens had filed petitions for two sites, one on the west edge of Crandall and another located supposedly at the district's geographic center. The board planned an April 9 referendum on these two sites, called, respectively, the Sterling and the Crandall sites (see figure 2). Davids urged his readers to select the Sterling site since it would cost $600 an acre compared to Crandall's $750.

At this same referendum residents would be able to vote on a name for the unit's high school. As Crandall High School, it called attention to only one of the five villages and irritated the sensitive West Siders. Voters had many names to chose from—Pentagon, Heartland, Five Points, Teen Acres, etc. Harmony was the winning name. This new name, the hopeful harbinger of a yet-to-be realized solidarity, was the only affirmative outcome of the April 9 vote, for on the remaining questions, "Should land be purchased?" "Should it be the Sterling site?" Should it be the Crandall site?" the district's answer was emphatically negative, although Killmer and Eaton decidedly favored not only buying land, but buying the Sterling site. They could not reject this clearly West Side site.

After the referendum, Davids asked his readers to keep uppermost in their minds the question, "What next? The only conclusion that can be reached is that Eaton and Killmer townships cannot depend upon District No. 110 to solve their school problem." He doubted that a new high school would ever be built because residents will not provide the money, yet he could not see how the board would solve the problem of overcrowding in the present high school. Overcrowding and the Sterling site were secondary issues for Davids; more profound and pressing matters animated him.

> They are taking high schools away from the smaller towns and now the proposal is to do away with the office of [township] commissioner of highways and put the authority in the hands of the city superintendent. This is probably only the beginning. Next will be a move to abolish the offices of [township] assessor and township clerk and thus the township units will not be needed. . . . [P]eople of the township will lose forever the freedom they have enjoyed for so many years.

Given this concern, we can be sure that Davids's reasons for rejecting the school-closing recommendations of the three-man

committee encompassed more than the inconvenience of busing and the added financial costs.

In their own way, the events of 1950 in Unit 110 promised
to be momentous. The newly named, newly organized Harmony High School brought together all the district's senior
high students for the 1949–50 school year. Oldham and Tipton
residents complained of the loss of their "social center" (the
high school), and Killmer joined Eaton in disparaging the
board's broken promise to schedule some of the high school's
athletic events in the different village high school gyms. One
Eaton merchant said his business declined after Harmony High
School opened in September 1949. Negative feelings escalated
and sentiment surfaced favoring a Killmer-Eaton secession
from Unit 110 and a union with each other. Sentiment became
action as each village organized its own meeting to thrash out
the issues and to vote whether to leave the school district.
Rumors that the high school building in Crandall would be
enlarged inflamed these feelings, because any improvement to
this building hinted at school board support for locating the
master high school permanently in Crandall. In Killmer, academic rationalists—those who viewed the continued development of Unit 110 as a promise of improved educational
quality—argued to no avail. The actual and impending sense
of loss was far more painful than the claim that Unit 110 gave
Killmer children the best education they ever had; no West
Sider at the time refuted this claim. Clearly, the issue was
joined at the point of loss, not of gain, reinforced by the doubt
that a truly centrally located school would ever be built and
by the belief that Killmer children had to travel too far in
attending Harmony High School.

Within one week in March 1950 the separatist resolve
moved toward a climax. At a public meeting in Killmer, residents voted 95-0 to detach and organize a new school district
comprised of Killmer and Eaton. This new school district
would preserve a K–6 school in each village and would build
a new junior-senior high school midway between the two villages. According to this plan, board members would be di-
vided—three to Killmer, three to Eaton, and one to Crawford

Township, parts of which also wanted to withdraw from Unit 110. When Eatonites held their public meeting, at which a vote of 85-8 favored secession, they insisted "that all persons desirous of becoming officials [school-board members] in this new district be in accord with its aims and objectives." By making endorsement of the status quo a condition for school-board membership, Eatonites intended to enshrine the status quo they hoped secession would maintain.

There were other banners in Page County besides those of Davids's *Killmer News*. The *Pageville Press* reported staunch support for preserving Unit 110 and questioned the magnitude of secessionist sentiment where it supposedly existed. The *Press* quoted an Eaton woman who asked, "Are we thinking of our children or are we more concerned with community rivalry? The high school students I know are happy." At any rate, Unit 110 loyalists in Eaton seemed never to mount a successful countercampaign; they failed to mobilize and resist the efforts of those who insisted that exit from the school district was the only alternative. They were heartened but not effectively inspired by Pageville College's professors of education and other well-wishers who assured Unit 110 residents that if they allowed their inexperienced school district one more year, their problems would be solved. Optimism did not characterize the observer at Eaton's public meeting who said, "A five-headed horse never did live. In Unit 110, each head wants to do the controlling."

Indeed, optimism was in short supply as it snowed and thawed and rained in March 1950, and a committee of secessionists laid their plans. First, the former Elm Place school district, whose one-room school had been swallowed up by the formation of Unit 110, would circulate a detachment petition among its twenty-five eligible voters. Second, if the Elm Place petition stood up in court, then this initial secession would be followed by the secession of Killmer, Eaton, and Crawford townships. The committee also rejected as "a stalling tactic" the school board's suggestion to appoint a group to study Unit 110's building needs: "There is no evidence Unit 110 can work and no reason to give it one more year." Unit 110's attorney,

Sam Miller, countered the secessionists with the board's determination to fight the Elm Place petition. Miller said the law allowing an area like Elm Place to detach was new and untested, and he questioned if the law was meant to allow a school district to be broken up. When twenty-three voters signed Elm Place's detachment petition (by law only a two-thirds majority was needed), it was ready for submission to the county court.

Words flooded Unit 110 following the Elm Place petition. Never mind that they had been spoken at too many previous meetings; never mind that the opposing sides talked past each other. The discourse had no chance to become an exchange because the situation in Unit 110 was like a debate in which contenders on two entirely different issues accidentally meet on the same stage. Having come together, they offer their respective arguments, ignoring the mismatch between their points. Nonetheless, while the court deliberated the Elm Place detachment, the debaters spoke out. In school district newsletters, Superintendent Trummel conveyed his position:

> Isn't it true? That Unit 110 has provided educational opportunities that have never previously been offered by any school in the unit? . . . That those who would have areas withdraw are promising no more than Unit 110 *now offers?* . . . That we gave our other type of school organization 25 to 50 years in which to make progress?

Trummel's point is clear: Give us a chance. You never had it so good.

Glenn Davids did not respond to Superintendent Trummel. Indeed, at no time did he address himself to the pro–Unit 110 case, for he, like everyone else, had his own to articulate. He restated the "our town will die" litany—without a high school, newcomers will refuse to buy houses in Killmer, property values and businesses will decline, income will drop, taxes will remain high, and the community spirit will dissipate. The recitation over, Davids took on the issue of educational quality:

> A good education is always desirable, but there are other things to be taken into consideration. When it is possible to keep our town alive [the "other thing" to be considered]

and at the same time to have an adequate educational system, then that seems the plausible thing to do.

Trummel had his answer. Keep your good education. We'll settle for adequate education if we can assure our town's survival.

Among those who defended Unit 110 was a group of citizens from within the secessionist townships who petitioned the court to deny Elm Place's request. The *Killmer News* had plain talk about the latter group's credentials to speak. They were not bad people, really, "gentlemen of good character." But "they have not accumulated any large holdings of land or money, which some seem to think is against them." Davids never was particularly subtle, least of all when he was being sniffish.

The last of the torrent of voices that poured forth following the Elm Place petition belonged to students; they sought the editorial columns of the *Pageville Press*.[3] For the most part, the argument for educational quality struck home with them. Detachment found at least one student supporter, inspired by the Twenty-third Psalm, concluding that, "Yea, though I walk through the valley of the shadow of Harmony High, I fear no education, for Unit 110 is with me. . . . Surely goodness and mercy shall deliver the western end from Unit 110 and we shall dwell in a school of our own forever." Another student answered this prayer for deliverance with:

> Unit 110 is my shepherd, but I lack parental encouragement to believe in it. It maketh me to earn my own grades; it leadeth me beyond the confines of beloved Eaton. It restoreth educational standards in Killmer; it leadeth me to greater endeavor for my future's sake. . . . But surely shortsightedness and misinformation shall deliver the western region from Unit 110, and we shall dwell in a condemned building in Eaton forever—or until the roof caves in.

In addition, eight graduates of Killmer High's last senior class wrote a collective letter to the editor. Their point: any improvement in Killmer's school is due to its connection with

Unit 110, the present secessionists are those who bitterly fought any forward step for as long as they could remember, and the school board is to be commended for its dignified response to often malicious critics. Their only complaint "is that Unit 110 wasn't set up years ago." The student perspective did not prevail. Their sense of academic gain was overwhelmed by the secessionist's sense of community loss.

The secessionist group, from spring 1950 until late fall 1951, focussed its attention not on editorial byplay but on the courts where arguments for and against the maintenance of Unit 110 became secondary to the legality of Elm Place's detachment petition. Here is the chronicle of events relating to the legal proceedings:

April 17, 1950
Judge Hoffman receives a petition with 194 signatures that protests splitting the school district. The president of the Unit 110 school board had signed first, followed by forty-two persons from Killmer and twenty-four from Eaton.

April 20, 1950
Judge Hoffman's transfer of the case to Judge Friedman delays the Elm Place petition hearing.

April 27, 1950
Judge Friedman hears testimony from Superintendent Trummel. He will offer his decision on May 1.

May 18, 1950
For the third time, Judge Friedman delays his decision. He is said to be waiting for a ruling from the state supreme court as to whether his court has the right to exercise discretion on the Elm Place petition.

May 25, 1950
Judge Friedman approves the Elm Place detachment petition. Now, in keeping with the plan of the secession committee, it is time for Killmer, Eaton, and Crawford townships to file similar petitions. Of 1,200 eligible voters in these three townships, 1,000 sign detachment petitions.[4]

May 30, 1950
Antisecessionists from Killmer and Eaton file appeals against Judge Friedman's ruling and thereby extend the case beyond July 1, the legal date for the start of a new school year. Thus no new school district can be formed for the 1950–51 school year. And because of their approved petition, any students residing in the Elm Place area will have to pay tuition to enroll in Unit 110 in the coming school year.

January 4, 1951
Judge Stanley of the circuit court reverses Judge Friedman's decision and Elm Place once again becomes part of Unit 110. Stanley explains that county courts do not have the authority to handle land-detachment petitions and that the only recourse for detachment is new state legislation.

January 18, 1951
The state supreme court upholds a 1949 law which authorizes county judges to make changes in school district boundaries.

January 23, 1951
Accordingly, Judge Stanley abandons his earlier decision and thereby reopens the case of Elm Place's detachment. He will withhold his final ruling for thirty days, the time allowed for appeals to the supreme court's ruling.

March 8, 1951
Judge Stanley now refuses to act on the Elm Place petition until the supreme court decides whether it will rehear a case on the constitutionality of the 1949 law.

June 18, 1951
Six citizens file a petition objecting to the withdrawal of land from Unit 110. This postpones the decision which was to have been made today until September 17, and effectively precludes the formation of a new school district for the 1951–52 school year.

September 23, 1951
The supreme court again rules that the 1949 laws are constitutional and this permits hearings to be scheduled on the

Killmer-Eaton detachment case. A hearing is set for October 17.

October 18, 1951
Judge Harker, now presiding over the case, continues the hearings until October 25.

October 25, 1951
Judge Harker continues the hearings until November 7.

November 7, 1951
Judge Harker continues the hearings until November 20, because counsel for the petitioners fails to appear.

November 25, 1951
Judge Harker denies the Elm Place detachment petition.[5] Having denied this first petition, there is no need to consider that of Killmer and Eaton.

And so ended the first determined effort of the West Side to secede, four judges, nineteen months, and a confusion of petitions and judicial deliberations later. The notion of "sides" had appeared frequently before this time. As far as Killmer and Eaton were concerned, sides had been chosen, defenses erected, and battles fought. Hereafter, only the newest of newcomers would fail to understand instantly a speaker's reference to the East Side or the West Side. The final act of the prolonged detachment drama passed virtually unnoticed in July 1952, when the county superintendent of schools arranged a meeting to discuss the disposition of Elm Place because it had not maintained a school for two years. Since no one appeared at this meeting, the county superintendent reassigned Elm Place to Unit 110.

Also in 1952, Glenn Davids sold the *Killmer News*, bewailing, as he relinquished his editorial forum, the public's lack of interest in school affairs.

The High School Site Issue (1949–56)

Over the extended course of defeat, secessionist ardor abated. Unit 110 received the additional year it had been urging the secessionists to grant in the hope that more time would give the district a chance to demonstrate its competency to resolve outstanding problems. In fact, the district got more than one year's grace, but to no avail, for its anguish would now be generated by another problem—where to build the new, master high school.

Throughout the secessionist period and beyond it, until May 1956, the site issue prevailed. Everyone agreed that Harmony High School was overcrowded but no majority could be found to support any proposed new site. In August 1949, the board launched a citizens' committee; the committee found the exact geographical center of the district (one-quarter of a mile northwest of Crandall); and, like a road show, moved its act from town to town for public hearings on a 6-6 or 6-3-3 plan. Believing it was timely to make a decision, the board in September 1950 asked 1,500 district patrons, by means of a post-card questionnaire, if they favored selection of a school site at the present time. Of the 378 cards returned, 89 answered yes and 289 answered no. Not one township affirmed a desire to make a site decision.

Eighteen months later, Superintendent Trummel put the site problem back in the news. He called a meeting of advisors to discuss a "permanent building program," especially his old 1948 plan of a K–6 school in each town and one 7–12 junior-senior high school in a central location. The school board's move to implement Trummel's ideas with a $1.5 million building program was followed by another move by Killmer to withdraw from the school district, its second such effort in four years. Trummel's building efforts were eclipsed during the four months Killmer took for detachment petitions to be signed and submitted to the county board and for the county board to dismiss the petitions on the ground that they lacked sufficient signatures.

This four-month detachment interlude stifled Superintendent Trummel's "permanent building program" and new site-selection and building plans did not emerge again until March 1954, when the *Pageville Press* announced, "Unit 110 Eyes $950,000 High School Building Vote." On April 10 voters would be asked to approve the money to build a new senior high school on the twenty-three acre Jordan site (a recent entry in the site battle). As it turned out, they approved none of the referendum's three propositions which, if passed, would have authorized the board to purchase the Jordan site, to build a new high school, and to issue bonds to finance the project. The margin of rejection was larger than that on any issue in the unit's short history; only Crandall supported the three propositions.

Since the need for more space and for repairs to existing buildings was indisputable, neither Superintendent Trummel nor the school board could take this message of rejection as the last word. A new referendum was called for November 19, 1955, in the first semester of Unit 110's eighth year. Voters were asked to respond to seven different propositions, more than on any previous referendum. Perhaps its strategy of a bone for everyone made the difference to the 1,854 voters who turned out to register what they thought Unit 110 ought to do about its bones. To no one's surprise, Crandall once more affirmed all propositions and Tipton overwhelmingly rejected them all. Still, there was a difference in this referendum. For the first time since the 1948 vote to establish the school district, there was at least a greater degree of affirmation, along with the usual rejection, in Killmer, Eaton, and Oldham. Their support, combined with Crandall's substantial approval, sufficed to carry some of the propositions; their rejection of other propositions was insufficiently large to cancel the effect of Crandall's sizeable approval. A weary superintendent and school board looked with satisfaction at these results:

Proposition 1
To build an addition to Eaton Grade School—1,067 yes, 676 no; rejected only by Tipton.

Proposition 2
To issue bonds for the Eaton addition—1,016 yes, 696 no; rejected by Tipton and Oldham.

Proposition 3
To issue bonds to repair and alter Harmony High School in preparation for its becoming a grade school—986 yes, 733 no; rejected by Eaton and Tipton.

Proposition 4
To issue bonds to repair and alter the grade schools in Tipton, Oldham, Killmer, and Crandall and the junior high in Tipton— 1,024 yes, 701 no; rejected only by Tipton.

Proposition 5
To build a new high school building—989 yes, 772 no; rejected by Eaton, Oldham, and Tipton. These results mark the beginning of a brief period in which Killmer and Crandall voted together to support major school board proposals.

Proposition 6
To issue bonds to pay for the new high school—947 yes, 802 no; rejected by every area but Crandall.

Proposition 7
To purchase the Jordan site for the new high school—869 yes, 875 no. Crandall's majority failed to overcome the negative votes of the other villages, and by six votes this crucial proposition failed. Thus, the site issue was unresolved.

At last, Unit 110 had a mandate to upgrade its elementary schools and to build its master high school, but without a site the high school building project once again had to be postponed. However, buoyed by its unprecedented success, the board went land hunting and within three weeks found four more potential sites all known by the names of their owners— Stone, Wagahoff, Tyndall, and Chalmers. They varied in their geographical relation to Crandall (and thereby being closer to the West or to the East Side); on or off a hard road (and thereby providing easier or harder automobile access to the proposed building); close to or far from state highway 79 (and thereby necessitating much or little school bus time on this busy road); and with or without an adequate water supply. A Citizens Advisory Committee, with the help of a consulting engineer's

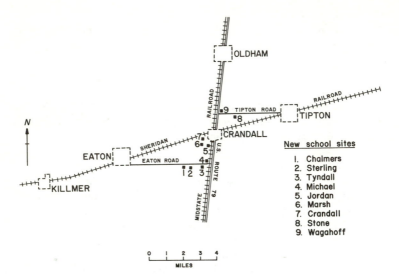

Figure 2.   Sites considered for Unit 110's new master high school, 1949–56

survey, examined all the new sites as well as the original Jordan site and voted 20 to 12 in favor of Jordan. The board approved this decision by a 4-to-2 vote, with Eaton's representative James Goodrich abstaining, and agreed to hold a referendum on January 21, 1956.

The six-vote defeat of the Jordan site in November 1955 widened to 68 in the January 1956 referendum; the totals were 1,103 yes and 1,171 no. Eaton's agitation brought out 420 more district voters than in 1955, with about half of the new voters coming from Crandall. Only Crandall approved the site.

With money for a new high school in hand (from Proposition 6), the board moved the district to a March 1956 vote on the Stone site. Of 1,724 voters, only 636 approved, with over 400 affirmative votes coming from Oldham and Tipton and substantial rejection coming from Killmer, Eaton, and Crandall. Taxpayer sensitivity in Tipton magically dissipated in the face of a site that was close to them and therefore acceptable. Two months later, with the money for a new school still in school board hands, 1,485 weary voters marched to the polls. This time Crandall and Killmer majorities sufficed to win the day for the Marsh site, seventh in a seemingly never-ending list of alternatives, by a vote of 762 to 723. The cornerstone for Harmony High School was laid on the Marsh site on November 11, 1957.

"Everybody went back home," one oldtimer recalled, "and we had peace for a few years. It lasted until Crandall outgrew its K–8 and Tipton got too small for its K–8." When the new high school opened in 1958, one era of confusion and conflict ended. Twenty years later a Unit 110 resident commented:

> They placed the new school out in the country where it was inconvenient for everyone. But, you know, there was a thousand and one reasons why it shouldn't be anyplace.

For the next four years (1958–62) Unit 110 experienced good times unmarked by the type of excitement that would send the West Side scurrying to its lawyers. At last, Superintendent Trummel attained a measure of tranquility for himself and his troubled school district. "I came to Unit 110 in 1958," said a former principal of Killmer Grade School. "Then there was no conflict. It seemed like those first few years the board, the principal, and the teachers were all one big happy family."

When Trummel fell ill in 1962 the school board made Assistant Superintendent Donald Gaumnitz the acting superintendent for 1962–63 and then the superintendent. Long an employee of Unit 110, Gaumnitz was no stranger to the divergent opinions espoused at the time of the school district's birth: we were doing well "until this reorganization popped up"; schools are for the benefit of children, not of adults; and without a school, Killmer is on its way to becoming a "ghost town." Later, when Gaumnitz would feel compelled to respond to financial pressures, he, too, would experience the ramifying consequences of these divergent opinions and be touched by the Chinese curse.

3

Before the Storm

Gaumnitz and Talman (1962–72)

Contemporary residents of Unit 110 look back at Donald Gaumnitz's superintendency as a time of peace and order, when wounds from the previous periods of turmoil had begun to heal and a semblance of order prevailed. Gaumnitz himself, though not given to the hyperbolic language of "golden ages," would assess his tenure as basically a positive time for Unit 110. Indeed, when the troubles of the mid- and late 1970s came, many residents openly wished for Gaumnitz's return to the superintendent's office. Few of those who commented on Gaumnitz and his work would mention the events that led him to resign, and those who did would do so in the gentlest of terms, as though his response to the events were an aberration. Gaumnitz sought no forgiveness; in his terms, what he did was not an aberration, but, rather, an attempt to maintain a viable school district.

Donald Gaumnitz was born and raised on a farm in central Illinois. In 1951, after one year of teaching elsewhere, he came to Unit 110. After teaching for five years, he was appointed principal, then assistant superintendent, and, finally, superintendent, all within a six-year period.

As we will soon be able to infer from Gaumnitz's first-person account of his seven-year term as superintendent

(1962–69), he was a determined man who knew what he wanted. His personal style gives no hint of ambition for high office or power. On the contrary, after resigning as superintendent, he quietly returned to the classroom to teach junior high school mathematics; he is reputed to be among the best teachers in the entire school district. As superintendent, he operated informally, rejecting a strict interpretation of those lines of authority which tend to hamper teacher-superintendent contact. And informality also characterized his approach to his school board. In that way which small towns have known for many years (and which disappears with increase of size and the coming of strangers who operate in more legalistic and technical modes), the board and the superintendent operated somewhat like a group of cronies who had long worked together and were well accustomed to each other's ways. Although then as now the public had access to the board meetings, Gaumnitz extolled the meetings of his day, when the public seldom was present and issues could be thrashed out in the privacy of a gathering of fairly like-minded persons.

Innovativeness was not a Gaumnitz hallmark. Yet when he saw a chance to enhance educational opportunity, he was secure enough to seize it. Accordingly, he began the shift of East Side children from school to school in what would resemble, by the mid-1970s, a game of checkers out of control (see table 6). His intent was to relieve the space pressure steadily mounting in Crandall and, at the same time, to group together larger numbers of children so that richer course offerings would be possible. When financial pressures joined space pressures, Gaumnitz moved doggedly to implement plans for new buildings and for centralization. These plans would mark his self-determined downfall.

Unit 110 did not so much reject Gaumnitz as it rejected his solution to its problems. He resigned well before his final year was over in order to facilitate the selection of his replacement. Donald Gaumnitz's style did not pave the way for easy acceptance of his successor, Jason Talman. Indeed, we must wonder what motivated the district's school board to select a man whose tenure in office would amount, at best, to a short transitional period of turbulence between Gaumnitz and Talman's own successor.

Donald Gaumnitz:
Unit 110 Superintendent (1962–69)

"In 1958 when they opened the new high school [Gaumnitz is speaking in August 1978], the superintendent moved me from Tipton to be principal at Crandall because he thought Tipton was dying and the job there would be a small one with a small number of people. I guess the town was dying, but you take Tipton's grocery store—it always was a little one-grocer thing, the type supermarkets easily kick out. It hasn't been that a high school's not there [that caused it to close]. In Killmer they say that when people go to Crandall to pick up their high school kids, they buy their loaf of bread in Crandall instead of in Killmer. Possibly. I don't dismiss the point altogether. I'm sure people look at the school situation when they come into a town thinking they might live there, but they also look at the sewage system, the water system, churches, distance to work, and a lot of other things. So I don't really think the school's the total situation by any means. But that was the point in everybody's eyes. They laid Tipton's dying on to the fact that people were moving into Crandall because the high school was there. And of course that's the argument Killmer has used all the way through.

"We transferred the seventh- and eighth-graders from Oldham to Tipton sometime around 1962. We did this so they'd have two teachers for each grade and be able to do a little departmental work. In 1963, I believe it was, we brought all the East Side's seventh- and eighth-graders into Crandall. We felt that by making one junior high for these three towns we could set up a program that would be more junior-high than grade-school oriented. I think you can attract a higher caliber of teacher to a larger school than you can when you have a small, shall we say, one-horse type school. Finances were a little part of the decision to bring the East Side together in one junior high in that we were duplicating. If we had a K–8 in each of the five towns, we had to buy five sets [of everything], one for each town.

"These organizational changes did not involve the West Side. As long as their kids went to school at home, they weren't that perturbed about educational opportunity. From the standpoint of educational opportunity, there's been a distinct difference between the East and West Side, because, well, frankly, on the West Side they are really not that concerned about education. [Judging from his comments below about Carrie Dewack and Eaton Grade School, he must have Killmer in mind.] Many times they've said they think the whole environment [of the student's home community] is more important than any opportunity gained by consolidation or any change like that.

"Now in Eaton they've been very fortunate because Carrie Dewack, their grade school principal, is a very strong individual. Carrie has probably a stronger program or as strong a program as you'll find in any school that size. She's been a very dominant and a very outspoken force in Eaton. You go on to Killmer. To me, Killmer's school has been weak; their administrators have been average; community involvement has been low from the standpoint of pushing for a library. Killmer has had more young teachers who have lived in Pageville and it's been more of just a job for them, whereas for the ones at Eaton, it's more like their school. Killmer sounds like Eaton when they talk about the importance of their school, but in Killmer things are more said than done. When Eaton says, 'We can do a better job educating kids in Eaton,' there's some basis.

"Years ago, when I was superintendent, the school board was a different kind of board than we have today. We never had those crowded board meetings. We seldom had to go into executive session. Back then we'd argue a point and when it was over we'd all go down to the bowling alley and have ice cream together before we went home.

"The only board member I'd say ever caused any problem was Denton Steed. First of all, Denton's ideas and mine were diametrically opposed. Secondly, Denton was a little slow on the uptake. In fact, he said once at a board meeting that the one thing he saw wrong with me was that when anybody asked a question, I had the answer too quick. I said, 'Well, that's what you're paying me for. If I don't have the answers, I shouldn't be here.' "

Steed was Killmer's board member. He, and also his wife, is mentioned several times in this chapter because his behavior is symptomatic of Killmer's out-of-step march with most of the school district. Among those who knew him, Denton Steed is as controversial today as he was in the past.

"In 1967 we moved [unsuccessfully] to centralize the junior high. I think we felt that we should be looking at a junior high program where all seventh- and eighth-graders had the same opportunities. I also felt that we ought to broaden the curriculum for our seventh- and eighth-graders because we offered just the basic four subjects and that's about it. At that time, we could have built a new building for a half to a third of what we can build it today. Hindsight. I've had people tell me who originally had gone against it, 'Well, we probably made a mistake.' But at that time, no way. Crandall was the only town that carried it in the referendum. Probably the main factor on the West Side was they didn't want their seventh- and eighth-graders to go out of town. On the East Side, I don't remember what the vote was, but I think they didn't want to spend more money, and they didn't want to build a new building in Crandall. If we had proposed building the new junior high at Tipton or Oldham, then they would have voted for it. You see, I don't think it was the concept of the junior high that was defeated; for some people it was the location."

Announced new plans in Unit 110 mean announced opposition will soon emerge. Gaumnitz's plan was attacked in Killmer by an ad hoc group called the Citizens for the Study of Education in Unit 110. They advertised the plan's adverse effects on athletic and music programs (fewer schools means fewer opportunities to participate) and its probable tax increases. And they argued that because "smoking, drinking, and sex are very difficult to control," their seventh- and eighth-grade girls do not belong on the same campus with senior high school boys, but "in their own communities, even if the school is smaller." To this implicit accusation Harmony High School students retorted, "Grossly unfair."

In fact, a burst of letters to the editor hit the newspapers. Killmer loyalist Ray Reinhart wrote that people who like small towns do not like their children to be lost in the shuffle of large, impersonal schools. And in what must be seen as audacity, given their community's orientation to maintaining the educational status quo, the board representatives of both Killmer and Eaton wrote, as earlier they had voted, in support of Gaumnitz's plan. Harry Willard, a respected farmer and Killmer's board member, said that the Killmer school building did not merit further repair and a centralized junior high promised quality education. Dora Thompson, Eaton's board member, shared Willard's view.

Following the referendum, the *Killmer News* expressed surprise at the outcome, because all signs had pointed to popular acceptance of the middle school plans—until Killmer and Eaton had organized to oppose it. Ever in support, Crandall's citizens alone gave a majority to the plan; otherwise, the response was overwhelmingly negative, hardly a vote of confidence to the man who as teacher and administrator had selflessly served the unit for so many years. Only 499 voted yes and 1,302 voted no. Killmer and Eaton voters turned out in the relatively large numbers that had usually distinguished them from voters in the other three areas. When necessary, they could always get out the votes.

At the next school board election, held several weeks after the lost referendum, Killmer and Eaton joined forces to defeat Harry Willard and to replace him with Denton Steed, who was known to oppose higher taxes and who would never support anything less than a K–8 school in Killmer. Steed became the opposition-in-residence for the final two years of Superintendent Gaumnitz's tenure, providing the single nay to the usual yeas of the six other board members.

The *Pageville Press* summed up a post-referendum meeting of concerned district citizens with words that epitomize the plight of this and many other periods in the school district's history. Indeed, the words could well be taken as Unit 110's epitaph: "It is realized that improvements must be made . . . but just what the patrons of the district can agree on remains to be seen."

"With the defeat of the referendum in 1967," Gaumnitz continues, "I knew I was not going to convince anyone that they ought to look at a centralized program. Throughout the 1968 school year I had in mind the idea that maybe they needed new blood. I'd been there seven years. So I resigned in January 1969 to give the board plenty of time to get a new superintendent. I hadn't been badgered by the community, no sir. Let me give an example. In the nine years that I worked as assistant superintendent and superintendent I had only one phone call at home that could be called a critical phone call. One. The woman was upset because I had jumped on the principal of her town and she was his close friend. I was critical of some of the things that he was doing."

There can be no doubt that people were critical of what Superintendent Gaumnitz had hoped to do. After Gaumnitz assessed the financial status of the district, the condition of its buildings, and the state of its curriculum, he concluded that a comprehensive building program was required. Ever cautious and conservative, Gaumnitz was not swayed by the currents of educational faddism, but he felt it was timely to build. District voters rejected his vision of change by considerably more than a two-to-one margin. Nonetheless convinced of the utility of his 1967 plans, he resigned and was replaced by a man of profoundly different style and disposition.

Jason Talman Takes Over, (1969–72)

Jason Talman no longer has a job in any school district, though for many years he was committed to public-school work and had advanced from teacher to counselor to principal to superintendent, following his father, who had been an educator for over forty years. Unit 110 represented a challenge to him of the sort that a larger school system makes possible, and Jason Talman is the sort of man who enjoys a challenge. Three years in Unit 110 convinced him that the good life was elsewhere; he found it in business and now wonders why he remained so long in education. In his present business office a table crowded with trophies attests to his competency as a salesman. After the travail of his superintendency, he may well have doubted his competency to sell anything at all since he could not convince Unit 110 residents to accept either his educational means or ends.

Jason Talman, speaking in the fall of 1976, describes his years as superintendent in Unit 110:

"When I was interviewed for the job, the board did not so much want my views on consolidation as they did on a junior high, but I felt like consolidation of the district was needed when I was hired. My first priority was to redecorate the superintendent's office. Then I was concerned with instructional programs and facilities below the high school level.

"I looked at all five towns as possible places to live. Killmer attracted me the most, but when I examined the grade school, I decided against Killmer. Their school was a firetrap and I wouldn't put my kids in it.

"Before I took the job, I got an intimation that something was going on in the school district. Denton Steed and his wife visited me in Hesselton where I worked. They were trying to cultivate me, to feed me a typical Killmer line: Killmer was not getting a fair shake, had hand-me-down equipment, etc. After I got on the job, I agreed. There'd been no life-safety work done, so their building was in the worst shape. The Killmer principal was the least aggressive of them all and he and Steed were on the outs. Steed spied on him and the school to check if people worked their proper hours. Later, the principal decided Mrs. Steed was not a good kindergarten teacher and she shouldn't be rehired. I agreed and so did the board.

"I'd say it was after about six months when people in the district began tracking me. Kept it up all the time I was superintendent and at least once after I left office and moved away. My wife and I would go out at night for a social evening and there'd be one of my trackers sitting in a car, looking to see who else was coming, and taking down all license numbers. Because we socialized with some board members, we were being checked to see if we had illegal board meetings.

"On our board, mostly we'd have a 6-1 vote; Steed voted against everything. Things were OK until some new people got elected. Then it got to be 4-3, and that's not my idea of how a board's supposed to operate. I expect a board to accept the superintendent's professional opinion regarding the best options available in a given situation. To my way of thinking, I come up with the options, they chose from among them, and then we close ranks to figure out a plan of attack. I thought this was where I was.''

In short, Talman thought his school board would operate in a certain way. It did not. Actually, Talman's decisions headed him into a storm that continued unabated throughout his tenure. In the name of his view of educational progress, he contributed to its fury.

In November 1969, the first semester of his tenure, the school board endorsed Talman's plan to move his office to a new location, demolish Killmer's old grade school and build a new one, provide an addition to all the other grade schools, and build a new districtwide junior high for grades 6–8 near the Harmony High School campus. Within thirty days of this endorsement, Talman was plunged into the politics of Unit 110. In December 1969 Dorothy Hammersley wrote a letter to the editor urging her fellow Killmerites not to sign the detachment petition then circulating in town because the Garrison school district (again suggested as the district with which Killmer should unite) could not possibly accommodate Killmer's students and, besides, Garrison had a higher debt rate than Killmer. Hammersley notwithstanding, the rumble of secession, though not heard for sixteen years, resounded once again. And in January 1970 Superintendent Talman took to the road, his verbal goods assembled, to assail Killmer and the other communities with his reaction to the events of the past few months. His opening remarks to the different communities acknowledged the signatures of 194 Killmer residents affixed to a letter that announced their intent to detach. After informing his listeners that he was cognizant of Killmer secessionist activity, he began his appeal. He noted that "Unit 110 has progressed very little in the past several years," and then asked, "Are you really going to vote against me? Are you going to vote against my plan? You have already pitched away a half-million dollars by not building in 1967. What bargain price would you have paid before that?"

While Talman was hustling support for his version of the grand plan, a new group had been organized which would occupy a central place in Unit 110 affairs for years to come. The group's major message was embedded in its name, Unit 110 Citizens for K–8 Schools; their name contained the yardstick with which they would judge new building plans, school board candidates, whatever. K–8—that was the crux. With a four-year, centrally located high school already an accomplished fact, that left Eaton and Killmer's kindergarten and eight elementary grades to keep secure. In short, the new group conceded the loss of the old village high schools, but they wished to encircle with a protective wall their intact K–8 grade schools and to reestablish them in the other three villages where they no longer existed. Thus the K–8ers, as they soon came to be called, promulgated a proposal in January 1970 that sought voter consent to build a K–8 school in each village based on a coordinated, unitwide curriculum. They wanted "equal opportunity to be provided for all elementary children, wherever they live." Talman and the board were not quite ready to entertain this proposal. Months later, feeling more desperate, they would look upon it more favorably.

Denton Steed announced his candidacy for reelection to the school board in February 1970. As a convinced K–8er, he highlighted his announcement with support for enriched grade schools *within* each community. The same day Steed publicized his candidacy, the *Killmer News* brought Killmer's current detachment efforts up-to-date: Killmer leaders had met with Garrison's school board and superintendent, and with architects and lawyers, in order to explore the feasibility of a merger with Garrison. The Garrison school board said it could not accommodate Killmer's high school students without a building addition, an addition would require a referendum, and since they had just passed a bond referendum, another one was unthinkable. Moreover, Garrison could not afford to accept Killmer unless Killmer brought its tax dollars with them in the first year they joined Garrison; the state school code precluded this. Accordingly, secession failed once again and Killmerites faced a year in which momentum gathered to support what they found, second only to the loss of their grade school, particularly abhorrent—a centralized junior high.

Unmoved by the strength of Killmer's reaction to his 1969 plans, Superintendent Talman drew up comparable ones for 1970. These received a 7-0 mandate from the school board. (Steed was defeated by Joyce Ellis, a write-in candidate supported by the East Side, and his nay vote was now gone.) For Talman, the critical fact was that the school system had increased its overall enrollment by 25 percent between 1962 and 1970, and it had not added a single room since the high school was built in 1958. High school classes met on the gym bleachers, and all the buildings were overcrowded. He and the board set November 14, 1970, as the time to vote on a referendum which Talman believed would put a "chicken in every pot"—a new grade school in Killmer, an addition to each grade school in the other villages, and a new centralized junior high in Crandall. To pave the way for an affirmative vote, Talman distributed an information sheet to all district residents which explained that "our district cannot afford to offer equal education with the small enrollment that we have in [so many] separate facilities." Talman's good intentions were rewarded by a degree of negativism unsurpassed since the agonizing series of votes in the 1950s to select a high school site.

The K–8ers attempted to rally support for a plan developed around a K–8 school in each village, a plan that purported to satisfy the space needs Talman and the board had been trumpeting. They enlisted everyone they could, including people who favored a centralized junior high but who joined the K–8ers in the district's intense and growing antagonism to Talman. In the face of mounting opposition to the referendum, the school board, shortly before the November 14 voting date, publicly asserted its unanimous support for Talman's plan. The day before the vote, county and local newspapers carried letters to the editor and full-page advertisements: Vote against the building program to "preserve your community school and save over $3,500,000 in taxes." Vote for the building program because "good schools improve communities."

If Talman's promised chicken in every pot did not bring voters flocking to him, it brought them to the polls in record numbers. Having put his talents of persuasion to full use, Talman was optimistic—until the returns came in: Oldham's margin of rejection was relatively small, but large negative majorities in Killmer and Eaton almost equaled the total positive vote from all five towns. Killmer did not bite at the lure of a completely new K–6 school. Only Crandall saw good things in the pot, though not by the one-sided margin of earlier referenda. The results recorded in table 8 show what each of the unit's many referenda has demonstrated—every village has a core group that will support superintendents and school boards in their quest to centralize and to consolidate, but that this sentiment is shared by only a minority of school district voters.

Seven years later, Herb Kostner, an Eaton board member in Talman's time, speaks bitterly of the referendum's defeat as he recalls that, "we worked our asses off." It was disheartening because

> the way it was defeated you'd have thought we were making a shot for the moon. I think I saw the only fist fight there ever was at a board meeting. Some of my own relations called me a son of a bitch [for supporting the referendum] and that's when I resigned. Anything that costs money you'll have trouble getting through, especially with farmers and landowners.

With two Talman-inspired failures in hand, the school board was prepared to listen to the Committee of Unit 110 Citizens for K–8 Schools. This was in January 1971, two months after Talman's rejected referendum. The K–8ers had enlisted an architect to draw up plans which they claimed would save money, provide adequate space, and preserve a K–8 school in each village. As a result, in a rare moment of accommodation to the West Side, the board basically approved the K–8ers' plans.

Accordingly, on March 3, 1971, the board announced a $1.98 million building program to be put before the voters on March 20. Talman again set his public relations machinery in gear. He published a newsletter which declared that Unit 110 ranked eighth in state wealth among the 126 school districts like their own, with an average daily attendance of 1,000 to 2,999, though it ranked only nineteenth in expenditures and ninetieth in tax rate. Talman meant to preempt the money issue as a basis for rejecting the referendum by demonstrating that in both absolute terms (wealth) and relative terms (tax rate), Unit 110 could afford his proposals. Unit 110's voters were not persuaded; fewer (1,621) turned out for the March 20, 1971, referendum than had for that of November 1970 or for Gaumnitz's 1967 referenda. Though the proportions were more favorable to this referendum, the distribution of votes took the familiar pattern of Crandall approval and of disapproval everywhere else; overall, 908 voted no and 703 yes.

Former board member Curt Smith, Eaton native and a founding member of the K–8 group, was disillusioned by the defeat of the March 1971 referendum:

> I [finally] realized that a lot of K–8ers, including the bankers in Crandall and Eaton, didn't want a bond issue passed because it would raise taxes. The big farmers in Killmer didn't want the program for the same reason. People just started making excuses about the building the board proposed to build in Killmer. I felt the board had bent over backward to appease us and do what the people wanted, but I was naive. I hadn't realized people were so against raising taxes and cared so little about education.

Superintendent Talman has a gentler recollection of the same period, notwithstanding that his views were the prime basis for the K–8 group's existence. He was fully aware of their concern for community identity and for their home-town businesses:

> They didn't realize that a school in town does not guarantee stores will stay in that town. A school didn't keep Killmer's drugstore open. "*Our* school, *our* ball team, *our* eighth-grade graduation"—it's there, it's real in their minds. As far as I'm concerned, it's justifiable, but economics dictates whether you get it or not. Economics and education take

priority over community. I never knew why Killmer and Eaton felt stronger about their identity than the rest of the district.

Community identity or taxes, community identity and taxes—Killmer and Eaton loyalists certainly were motivated by both factors, but depending on the issue, one or the other could be controlling. With the centralization issue stripped away in this latest referendum, the tax issue became primary. Cynics might say that the underlying reason to reject all building plans is financial, and that other, more acceptable reasons are advertised to cover up the crass dollar rationale. Indeed, the cynics might add that cost factors motivated both those who favored centralization and those who opposed it. The former believed that consolidation and centralization would save money by reducing the number of buildings, administrators, and custodial staff, but what they advertised was the prospect of academic gain. The latter believed that consolidation and centralization necessitated a building program that would cost money, and what they advertised was the prospect of community loss.

Years later, when they were again involved in a consolidation and centralization controversy, Killmerites would explain their seemingly capricious rejection of the 1971 plan—a plan that promised to secure their K–8 community school—in terms of the unacceptability of the package in which the promise was included. *If* they could have had a secure K–8 school in their old building, and *if* other building plans had not been included in the package, then they would have approved the referendum. Cynics also might accuse some K–8 supporters of looking for a dodge to avoid a tax increase at any cost. Well might Curt Smith be disillusioned.

The April school board election that followed the defeated March referendum added two Talman antagonists to a board which customarily supported him 6-1 or 7-0. Both new members were elected with K–8er's support, in their first direct effort to shape Unit 110 politics.

After the April 1971 school board election, things fell apart. At the first of two meetings in April, the board dismissed Alice Steed, Denton Steed's wife and Killmer's kindergarten teacher, and several other teachers. The board's second meeting in April was held in the high school auditorium because its agenda included a discussion of the dismissed teachers. Talman and the board knew their usual meeting room, with its capacity of seventy-five persons, could never contain the mass of angry residents who intended to hear the board consider this item. Newspaper estimates of the number present ranged from four hundred to seven hundred. Talman loyalists sported hand-printed tags declaring, "I support my school board," and Talman antagonists called for explanations, since none had been offered, to justify the dismissals. Soon after the meeting got started, newly elected board member Fred Parke (Crandall) accused Talman and the board president of "withholding information concerning decisions that I'm expected to vote intelligently on." This would be Parke's theme until Talman left Unit 110. Despite protests, pleas, and exhortations, the board upheld its previous decisions with a 4-2 vote, still refusing to disclose its reasons for dismissing the teachers. The minority votes came from Parke and Gargan (Tipton), the new K–8-supported board members. The missing member was Herb Kostner of Eaton, who soon afterward resigned in disgust, following criticism from his Eaton constituents for being a Talman supporter.

Reflecting what they felt was arbitrary procedure by Talman and the board in the teacher-dismissal cases, the Harmony Education Association sent Talman a letter of no confidence in May 1971. This was not necessarily his last straw, but Talman's departure from Unit 110 came before his third year (1971–72) as superintendent was complete. Soon after the school district's 1971 Christmas break, Talman warned district residents that the school system was on the verge of serious financial problems, and then he submitted his resignation. He had had enough. School-board legitimation of his resignation was upheld by a 3-2 vote.

Before the school year ended, Fred Parke, Talman's prime antagonist, was elected board president. In June 1972 Warren Hart replaced Jason Talman as Unit 110's superintendent.

Jason Talman recalls his departure from Unit 110:

> I still had a board majority of 4-3 in my favor till I left. We went through an exercise one night. They made a motion to rehire me even though the four knew I wouldn't stay, and they voted 4-3 in my favor, but I didn't change my mind.

In fact, Unit 110 is not distinguished by much changing of minds. It seems that at the outset of the unit's formation a script was prepared which would maximize dissent, perversity, and conflict. Except for brief lapses, it has been followed slavishly.

By the time Talman left office, Unit 110 and the world had changed significantly since that day in 1945 when the state legislature set in motion a process that created many new school districts. The high public expectations of the immediate postwar period had been undermined by the enduring cold war, the hot war in Korea, a tense balance of power between the United States and the Soviet Union, a costly competition for third-world support, and the disastrous conflict in Vietnam. Within the school district, important demographic changes had occurred. As we have seen (table 1), total district population had increased 20 percent, from 5,521 in 1950 to 6,977 in 1970. New subdivisions brought new people; new shopping centers and superhighways brought school-district residents increasingly to Pageville for shopping, work, and recreation; and a punishing annual inflation took its toll on Unit 110's finances. Yet, the more things changed, the more they stayed the same. Warren Hart inherited Jason Talman's recently remodeled office and his mantle of distress. Hart soon made it his very own.

4

Into the Storm
Hart Takes Over (1972–76)

Jason Talman's departure from Unit 110 was not an occasion for tears; indeed, Talman himself was glad to be gone. He had tried hard, meant to do well, and failed. The school district greeted Warren Hart with relief and anticipated that things would get better. Beginnings are like that when they follow a period perceived as disorderly—people welcome the new man, perhaps even welcome his new broom. The new man may share these same sentiments, both pleased to be rid of the problems of his previous job and eager for the chance of a fresh start. "I believe Unit 110 can be the finest school system anywhere," Hart announced soon after he took office. Hart's manner was pleasant, warm, and engaging; six feet tall and slightly overweight, he appeared solid and reassuring, the sort of person you would not readily push around. Warren Hart hoped to be reassuring and neither tried nor wanted to push anyone around. Advised of his predecessor's shortcomings, he meant to set things right by establishing public relations as his priority for the year. Contrary to Talman, who had been accused of running the district from his office, Hart told his secretary not to look for him before 10:00 A.M. because he would be out visiting people in the five communities. He also announced an open-door policy, urging people to come in and criticize: "You

may not always get what you want, but at least I'll listen."
Hart inherited a school board split between those who supported Jason Talman and those who sought to chase him out
of office; he inherited old school buildings and a clientele both
devoted to these buildings and opposed to the increase in educational taxes needed to maintain them; and, not least, he
inherited a school district with an East-West cleavage that at
times threatened to break it in two. Nonetheless, Hart had his
grace period. It lasted through January 1973, when the board
unanimously thanked him for the superior job he had done.
Thereafter, it was an embattled Hart who ran an embattled
school district. He remained superintendent until spring 1977.
When I met him (eighteen months before he resigned to take
another job), he welcomed my interest in Unit 110 and hoped
I wouldn't mind if he came to see me from time to time because
he occasionally needed to get away and talk, especially after
a board meeting. Board meetings, Unit 110's biweekly sessions
in the lions' den, were the arena for Hart's continuing anguish.

Hart, like Talman and Gaumnitz before him, felt compelled
to find ways to save money; total district assessed valuation
had peaked at $52.5 million in 1969–70, three years before Hart
came to Unit 110; and an annual decline in student enrollment
meant ever less state aid. After being on the job for approxi-
mately half a year, Hart took the occasion of the February 8,
1973, board meeting to unveil his plan to revamp the district.
It was a modest plan, directed only at the West Side, and would
provide the savings from one principal's salary. It placed all
their K–4 children in Killmer and all their 5–8 children in Eaton,
with one principal supervising both buildings. The board approved this plan by a 4-2 vote, and the West Side received its
first Hart-inspired cause for alarm. More immediately critical
to Warren Hart was—at this very same meeting—the board's
4-2 rejection of a teacher he recommended the district hire.
Because of this rejection, Hart complained, "Our administration means nothing. . . . We cannot continue to operate this
way." Hart was serious. He felt that the board's decision signified its rejection of his judgment on personnel, that it was a
vote of no confidence.

Hart soon demonstrated his responsiveness ("indecisive-ness," his detractors would call it) to the wishes of the district's citizens. At one of the March board meetings, having received enough phone calls to be satisfied that his February 8 internal reorganization plan was unacceptable, he urged the board to postpone such plans for one year. The board agreed. And he demonstrated the limits of his tolerance to the board's public rebuffs. How soon one falls from grace in Unit 110! Following its criticism of his work on the next year's contracts for the school district's principals, he asked the board to buy up the re-maining year of his own contract so he could resign on July 1. "For the betterment of the district and of Unit 110," Hart announced, "the board needs a superintendent they have faith in." Thirty sec-onds of silence followed his announcement. Then the board merely moved on to other business and the matter of Hart's future in Unit 110 was dropped for the time being.

These flareups and postponed plans were without apparent implications for the district, since in the April 1973 board elec-tion the three candidates ran unopposed and the total voter turnout was 380, down dramatically from the 1,200 of the 1972 election, when Jason Talman was the issue. Because Unit 110 residents do not stay home at election time unless they are reasonably pleased with the status quo, we may interpret this low voter turnout as a sign of their basic contentment. Further reinforcing the impression of district quietude was the board's February 1974 extension of Hart's contract for an additional two-year period and an even lower turnout for the April 1974 board election.

Thus Hart survived his first two years as superintendent under conditions relatively free from turmoil and rancor, but, to his and the board's discredit, free also from any exploration of the disagreements over the superintendent's role, school-board procedure, and school-district policy (especially relating to finances, internal reorganization, and centralization) that on several occasions had brought the superintendent and the school board, and the school board and the West Side, to sword's points. Though Hart survived these two years, he never worked out any effective modus operandi with the seven school-board mandarins.

In August 1974, just before the new school year was to begin, the board met to consider, in addition to its usual agenda items, several options regarding Tipton Grade School. Of all the five communities in Unit 110, Tipton alone had a declining population. Its large building, once the home of a bustling K–12 system, grew quieter each year; its third grade now had only nine students. Superintendent Hart proposed a number of alternatives, none of which pleased board member Arnold Clore (Oldham) who said that a more thoroughgoing plan of reorganization should be considered. "It's a matter of economics."

The board chose the most conservative alternative when it voted 6-1 to keep the class open by transferring two students to Tipton; Parke cast the sole negative vote. But Clore was right—it was a matter of economics. Superintendent Hart reported a deficit budget for 1974–75 in the district's education, transportation, building, and fire prevention and safety funds.

Hart was convinced that the district's financial problems could be resolved by closing schools. But he was ambivalent, then and later, not about what he should do, but about what he could do. He believed in the virtues of consolidation but at the same time knew that the West Side would resist any attempt to consolidate. Nonetheless, in search of a solution Hart arranged a festival of figures and proposals. In July 1974 his board hired a professional group, the Architectural and Engineering Service Corporation, to study Unit 110's financial and building problems and to report back to the board in December. Unwilling to wait for this report, Hart and his administrative staff, met several times between July and December and prepared a series of memorandums to the school board: October 30's "Plans for Future Years" set forth the balance in the education fund (a $291,000 balance in 1969 reduced to $33,000 in 1973); showed the increase in staff size (from 109 faculty in 1969 to 127 in 1973); and presented salaries as a proportion of total expenditures (38 percent in 1969 and 70 percent in 1973). He concluded that Unit 110 was fast approaching that point whereat no school district can maintain a balanced budget.

October 31's "Reorganization of District" set forth several
plans, including one for a K–8 building on each side of the
district that would reduce the present 82 teachers to 53; and
a K–12, one-campus arrangement, that would eliminate 27
teachers and 4 administrators. These were some ideas to
"brainstorm" about, Hart informed the board. November 5's
"Present Organizational Pattern," the third salvo within one
week, invited the board to ponder:

1. Can we afford an administrative cost per student that
   ranges [among the schools in the five villages] from
   $45.80 to $97.30?
2. Can we afford a student-teacher ratio that ranges from
   12.82:1 to 17.31:1?
3. Can we afford instructional costs per student that range
   from $594.74 to $919.87?

He followed up this effort with the announcement of an anticipated year-end deficit of $250,000. Hart showed himself to be
Gaumnitz and Talman's heir apparent with his conclusion that,
"We have reached our [financial] limit, unless we are willing
to centralize." And centralization was the order of the day in
the architectural consultant's report that was delivered in time
for the December board meeting. Each of their four alternative
plans called for closing either all or most of Unit 110's existing
primary schools and centralizing all their seventh- and eighth-
graders in a single school. Aswarm with options, the fancies
of several different groups, the school board turned away from
the products of Hart's endeavor toward its own perverse preference. First, the board approved a centralized junior high
school. Second, and most telling in terms of its implications
for Unit 110's leadership, the board rejected all the alternatives
posed by the school district's administrative staff and, guided
by Fred Parke (Crandall), endorsed a plan that required closing
the grade schools in both Tipton and Killmer. The decision was
upheld by a 4-3 vote at the February 2, 1975, meeting. "It is
politically unwise to close Tipton and leave the other [Killmer]
open," Parke explained, in the course of the discussion about
what plan to adopt. "It does not face the problem." What

"problem" he has in mind here he clarifies later in his own words. By its approving vote the board initiated several years of continuous disorder in Unit 110.

Newspaper headlines dramatized the school board's decision to centralize the junior high school. Village councils passed resolutions, and residents organized mass meetings to discuss their opposition to this decision. As in the past, letters to the editor and to board members underscored the extent of and the seriousness of the opposition. His ear ever to the ground, Hart heard and acknowledged broad district support for a K–8 school in each village; in the face of resistance, he was ready to retreat from the board's latest plan. Yet in the April 1975 board election, of the three board members who ran on a K–8 platform, only Harry Walter of Eaton won. This election contrasted strikingly with that of 1974 in that voter turnout rose from a record low of just over 300 in 1974 to a record high of 2,287 in 1975, almost double the number who came to the polls in 1972 when Jason Talman was the cause célèbre. Fred Parke of Crandall was reelected, as was Sarah Coler of Tipton.

Following the election, with the school closers enjoying at least a one-vote majority, Superintendent Hart turned to the practicalities of what now seemed unavoidable and imminent—closing Killmer's grade school. He did this with misgivings, his conviction shaken by the worried outpourings from Killmer and Eaton. Notwithstanding board president Arlberg's public admonitions that he would like to "see the board instruct Mr. Hart . . . to stop polarizing the communities and especially the students against the junior high concept," Hart sent the board a memorandum proposing an alternative reorganization plan—a K–6 in Killmer, a K–8 in Eaton, Tipton's grade school to be closed. Fred Parke reacted: "I am unhappy with the alternative. The board gave the administration a direction—a centralized junior high school." Parke was unhappy with Hart's alternative because he wanted not only a centralized junior high, but also an East-West quid pro quo: if the board closes a school on one side of the district, it must close a school on the other. Warren Hart temporized: "We need to take more time to study these proposals and do more talking." This exchange occurred at the May 15, 1975, board meeting; one week later, many Killmer and Eaton parents picketed and kept their children out of school. Eaton's involvement in this boycott stemmed from the prospect of its children's attending junior high school in Crandall, Killmer's from the loss of its grade school. Tipton, similarly affected, made no public protest at all.

Two hundred district parents crowded into the ordinarily ample space of the boardroom for the May 22 board meeting. They participated in three and one-half hours of acrimonious debate about the board's previously approved plans. At 11:00 P.M., board member Harry Walter (Eaton) moved to "rescind the junior high school for 1975–76, [leaving] the East Side [Tipton grade school] as it is this year and Eaton and Killmer as it is." Only Walter and Joe Kellog (Killmer) voted yes on this status quo motion. Then Kellog moved for an eighty-cent tax increase; though Walter seconded the motion, only Kellog supported his own motion. Kellog would consistently take the position of retaining Killmer's school and at the same time endorse efforts to redress the district's financial difficulties. Mrs. Norton, an Eaton resident, took a similar position in her letter to board president Herbert Arlberg. Her horse-trading offer was gently put—we will support the district's money efforts if you will acknowledge our "instinct to protect the young" [by leaving Eaton's junior high students in Eaton]. The board ignored the size of the crowd and Mrs. Norton's letter, and it prepared to reckon with Eaton and Killmer's Unit 110 Action Committee, which hired a Pageville law firm to search out any conceivable legal basis for unseating their antagonist board members.

Mrs. Norton's letter, the Unit 110 Action Committee, the Pageville law firm, and numerous calls to Tom Middle, Educational Service Region (ESR)[1] Board superintendent, for help in getting the school board to reverse its 4-3 school closing decision—all these created a tense climate in Unit 110. But as of June 1975 they had all failed to deflect the board. They failed again in July. And in most of August. Like a broken record, motions to return seventh- and eighth-grade students to the West Side and to reopen Killmer Grade School were put before the board twice a month. They garnered the votes only of Walter and Kellog. By late August, however, the West Side's Action Committee had found its solution. Their sleuths simply counted pupils and calculated the number of square feet per pupil that would be available in Crandall Junior High School for the 1975–76 school year. They reported their findings to ESR Board Superintendent Middle who, in turn, presented his view to Unit 110's school board: Crandall Junior High falls short of the legally required number of square feet per pupil. Fred Parke and Arnold Clore refused to change their vote, but they were swamped by a 5-2 majority that opposed opening a centralized junior high school for the 1975–76 school year.

The West Side's celebrated tape-measure victory could not alter one critical fact: the district still faced financial problems. Throughout the fall 1975 semester the level of Unit 110's storm increased. Unsure what to do, the board created a Citizens Advisory Committee (CAC) which, at least, would deflect attention from itself and give the impression it was doing something positive and concrete. And then the storm once more raged with fury. On February 2, 1976, the board's 5-2 vote again closed the entire school in Killmer and all but the third grade in Tipton. All West Side K–6 children would go to Eaton and their seventh- and eighth-graders to Crandall. For this, as for most other votes, Homer Gargan joined the four farmowner members who favored policies of consolidation and centralization as essential to quality education and fiscal responsibility. Moreover, the board decided not to extend Superintendent Hart's contract beyond July 1, 1978, its scheduled termination date.

"Save our School" announced the handouts distributed widely by the newly formed Killmer Concerned Citizens (KCC) organization. Killmer had declared war. At the KCC's February 12 meeting, the Killmer gym, normally echoing to the sounds of cheering children, was packed with the childrens' parents, who cheered KCC president Ray Reinhart and his soft-spoken but determined attempts to mobilize Killmer residents. Following this meeting, and continuing thereafter for weeks, the school board received letters from the Killmer Community Bank, the Killmer Women's Club, and numerous Killmer residents:

> I don't want to see my kids on a damn bus.
> Adults need the school as a community focal point in their lives.
> An important factor in a child's education is that he learn, "This is where I belong. This is my community. I am one of these people. . . ."

Killmerites reached the same end point—opposition to the closing of their school—from different directions: concern about the busing of their young children, about loss of business, about lowering of real estate values, about the faulty discipline, etc., of larger schools. No matter that their paths varied, they united, and remained united, for the long campaign to "save our school." In meeting after meeting they spurred on their Killmer Concerned Citizens group and surrounded the board members at their meetings with a dense ring of hostile, resentful parents. Moreover, they financed the KCC's activities with a succession of chili suppers and bake sales, and, when the time came, voted and signed petitions in record numbers. Over the next several years, Ray Reinhart and his KCC officers followed up their February 12 gym meeting with many others, persistently and tirelessly resisting Unit 110's school-closing policy.

Reinhart told the school board, "You voted to do something that will harm our kids in the most important years of their education. We feel our community is part of their education, so they shouldn't be in someone else's community." This is Reinhart's reaction to the prospect of Killmer children's being sent to the grade school in Eaton, their long-time West Side ally. Alliance notwithstanding, the geographic-political line that separated them became a boundary of tangible social consequence when Killmer children were destined to be educated in Eaton. The boundary, in Reinhart's terms, set apart people who in some sense constituted separate groups.

Over the next several months a verbal counterpoint developed from the outpourings of the various groups involved—the Killmer Concerned Citizens, the Citizens Advisory Committee, and the school board. Each group became a forum for the testing of ideas in response to the variant constituencies they imagined they served; in time, each group would be accused of serving selfish ends, of ignoring the realities of the district, of deserting their constituents, or worse. Of course, the critical forum remained the school board meeting, for it was here that the motions were made and the votes taken that decided the fate of a school. The Citizens Advisory Committee met frequently and talked at length. Its members strove to look beyond the immediate situation in order to take the fullest possible account of the educational, financial, and political realities of Unit 110; though appointed by the board, they refused to be subservient to it. In contrast, the Killmer Concerned Citizens were the special-interest group par excellence, its officers having been chosen to lead the assault on the enemy's fortress and secure the threatened jewel in Killmer's crown—a functioning K–8 school. The KCC lobbied at board meetings and elsewhere; at their own meetings they deliberated, agitated, and raged; feeling besieged, they responded with intensity to the latest, unthinkable acts of, in their opinion, a hostile, wrong-headed school board.

A Spring Chronicle (1976)

March 11, 1976: School Board Meeting
Kellog (Killmer): I move to rescind the closing of Killmer school.
Walter (Eaton): Second.
Coler (Tipton): Is that all you want is to open Killmer school? Don't you want to wait until the CAC make the report they've been working on so long?
Kellog: I don't want to wait because I've listened to people from Killmer and Tipton and they want a school in their town.

Coler: Don't you feel like if the board made a decision you should stand behind them?
Kellog: No.

To Kellog's motion, Mrs. Coler added an amendment that called for opening Tipton's school, as well. Then, in one of those sequences that would confound all observers, the board in a rare moment of unanimity voted 7-0 to add Tipton to Kellog's motion. It followed this vote with a 5-2 decision to reject both the motion and the amendment, with Mrs. Coler joining the majority to reject both her own amendment and Kellog's motion.

March 15, 1976: KCC Open Meeting
Kellog: The closing day [for Killmer Grade School] is May 27. They'll board up the windows and distribute the furniture to other schools. These are things I don't like to say before a friendly group. The only possibility to open the school is CAC, because the board says they'll listen to CAC's ideas. Meanwhile, the day after school closes, they lock the doors, winterize the building, board windows, and move furniture. Next fall, the kids'll get picked up at eight points beginning at 6:45. [The audience groans.]
Reinhart: I suggest we discuss the results of our survey on the five courses of action, taking one at a time.

The gymful of seething Killmerites discussed the five options. For number one, accepting the board's decision, there was no discussion, only derisive laughter. For number two, work within the district (by changing the makeup of the school board), they concluded that it would take too long and the results would be uncertain. For number three, create a dual district, that is, with separate school boards, one for the high school and one for Killmer Grade School, there was interest but doubt about its feasibility. For number four, join Eaton in an independent school district, there was considerable interest, but the sentiment that ultimately prevailed was, "Eaton's school is not threatened. This is our problem and this is what we have to face." For number five, detach from Unit 110 and annex to Garrison, there were no dissenting expressions; it clearly was the choice of the KCC's officers. It got 245 votes and aroused the evening's only round of applause. In fact, the KCC Withdrawal Committee, organized even before the voting tallies were announced, distributed a report describing the main task of initiating the withdrawal process—obtaining the signatures of two-thirds of all eligible voters on a detachment petition. It further acknowledged that Garrison, the school district to which Killmer hoped to annex, had a tax rate of $3.4238 per $100 assessed valuation compared to Unit 110's $2.4516. This is a significant difference to a cost-conscious village, but the report contrasted the losses of staying in Unit 110 (their grade school and the harmful influences of a centralized junior high in Crandall) with the gains of joining Garrison (retaining their K–8 grade school, improved educational programs, and association with a more compatible community). Finally, the publicity committee announced that it would soon sell bumper stickers which say, "Freedom in '76. Keep our school in town. No busing around."

March 22, 1976: KCC Open Meeting

It had been six weeks since the school board voted to close schools as a way to save money. Killmer residents, desperate to reverse this decision, had donated about $600 to support the KCC, most particularly to pay the fees of Farris Herbst, its Pageville-based lawyer. Herbst examined several likely KCC responses.

Herbst: Be pragmatic, ladies and gents. There's lots of ways to go at this, but you should exhaust all possibilities before you throw in the towel. I'll start off as a politician. You have the April 10 board election and one vulnerable member—Arnold Clore. I've got nothing against him, but he voted wrong. He can be beat. If you do that, you won't need my service. I wouldn't worry about a tax referendum or withdrawal [from Unit 110] until after the election. Defeat Clore and demand a new vote [to reopen the schools]. If you lose the election, then resort to other means. My

understanding is Crandall wants everything in Crandall.
We'll scrutinize the minutes to check out the legality of
everything. If I were in your shoes, I'd prefer to thumb
my nose at Unit 110 and detach to go to Garrison. If you
think Unit 110 can never be harmonious, then you should
detach.''

Herbst clearly reinforced Killmer's already strong sentiment
to secede from the school district, though he carefully characterized the choice of reconstituting the school board with
persons congenial to keeping village schools open. He did not
mislead Killmerites into thinking they would have an easy or
an inexpensive time with either a detachment or an electoral
route. In fact, he estimated that if a detachment petition
reached the state supreme court, it could cost about $7,000 in
legal and other fees.

March 25, 1976: School Board Meeting
in Killmer Grade School Gym
Each year the school board holds one of its regular meetings in each of the five villages. From Killmer's point of view,
it was most timely that the board came to Killmer when it did
because Killmerites felt abused; unaware of having done anything wrong, they could not fathom their school board's decision unless it intended to punish them. The board members
arrived at Killmer Grade School by 8:00 P.M., strode down to
the gym floor, and sat in metal folding chairs arranged around
a square formed by rectangular folding tables. The U-shaped
crowd surrounding them pressed in close like spectators at a
boxing match, their distress expressed on large banners fas-
tened to the gym walls: "Crandall K–12 Never"; "Closing of
Killmer Grade School—Watergate #2"; "Don't Bury Us
Alive"; "Parents Care—Why Doesn't the School Board?";
"Bigger Isn't Always Better." It was a spirited, pugnacious
audience that heard the Reverend Mr. Gaston of Eaton address
the board on behalf of the ministers of Unit 110's churches;
his brief presentation and the board's response would mark
this as a memorable occasion.

Gaston: As servants of the Word of God, [he read from his prepared text], we want to be counted as speaking with one voice. We think it is . . . important for you . . . to speak with one voice on the important issue of your motion to close Killmer and Tipton schools. We therefore respectfully request that a referendum be made to the voters [asking] ''Shall there be an education center in each village of Unit 110 . . . ?'' and that the board agree to determine its Education Program in accordance with the results of this referendum.

President Arlberg called for a roll call and the audience applauded the board's 5-2 decision to hold a referendum on April 10, 1976. Parke and Clore provided the two nay votes. Arlberg's aye vote, though it did not make a critical difference, surprised even himself.

April 10, 1976: School Board Election and
Referendum
April 10, 1976, became the spring focal point for Unit 110 residents, since Kellog of Killmer and Clore of Oldham were standing for reelection on this date, and Gaston's recommendation that there ''be an education center in each village in Unit 110'' was also on the ballot. The Committee for Community Schools ran large ads urging voters to support Kellog and Bill Kucera, a candidate from Eaton (which already had Harry Walter as board member). Kellog and Kucera, the ad exclaimed, stood for a school in each town, whereas Clore favored a costly centralized K–12 campus that would require massive busing. Oldham residents, seeing Clore in possible jeopardy, invoked the old gentleman's agreement that stipulated there always should be one school board representative for each of Unit 110's seven townships; this agreement had never been broken since the unit's inception. Although ''Concerned Parents of Oldham'' and ''Citizens for Clore'' responded in the press with a vigor not typical of the East Side, their efforts failed. Killmer and Eaton voters outnumbered Crandall, Oldham, and Tipton voters by 243 and easily carried

the day for Kellog and Kucera, as well as for the community-school referendum. The overall total of 2,333 voters surpassed the previous record of 2,287 set in the 1975 board election. Killmer and Eaton voters took advantage of their chance to elect two candidates, Kellog and Kucera, who supported K–8 community schools; by electing Kucera, they broke the twenty-seven-year-old gentleman's agreement. Clore clearly was the East Side's preferred candidate; yet it is important to note that a combination of Clore's outspoken, single-campus, K–12 vision for Unit 110 and Kucera's school-in-each-village platform swung 178 votes to Kucera from Clore's own East Side. Had these 178 persons voted for Clore rather than for Kucera, Clore would have won the election by 13 votes.

That Clore stimulated some negative reactions in his own village and township is also verified by the results on the informational referendum which invited residents to answer the question, "Should there be an educational center in each town?" Oldham voters voted yes 144 to 113; that as many as 113 negative votes were cast, however, testifies to Clore's strength at home. Only in Crandall did the community-school concept fail to be endorsed: there the vote was no by a margin of 327 to 167. Outside of Crandall and Oldham the yes vote was overwhelming, and the final result was 1,658 to 539. Since this was only an informational referendum, it did not enjoin the school board to do anything it had not been doing all along.

At the first, postelection board meeting, Bill Kucera of Eaton replaced Arnold Clore, farmer, churchgoer, father of seven, Oldham Township native, and Unit 110's most experienced board member. Having worked very hard for the school district, he wondered, "Why can't people let us do the best job we know how?" To Clore, the fiscal rationalist, the home-town schools were outmoded. "The major decision for a board member is how we can best use our tax money to educate the kids."

April 29, 1976: School-Board Meeting

At this first regular meeting following the election, Kucera joined Walter of Eaton and Kellog of Killmer in the new West

Side lineup of community-school supporters. Opposing them were Parke (chosen as the board president), Arlberg, and Gargan. Sarah Coler generally had joined these three (along with the now-defeated Arnold Clore) to provide the necessary majority to close and keep closed the schools in Killmer and Tipton. Coler was somewhat sympathetic to the community-school idea. She also was mindful of her constituent voters' sentiment in the comparatively passive village of Tipton and thus was torn between pleasing her patrons and doing what she felt was the financially responsible thing. East Side strategists calculated that they might lure her to their side, but she did not show up for this meeting. The meeting was highlighted by a Kellog-Parke dialogue. Kellog, predictably, moved to open Killmer Grade School and increase the educational tax rate. Parke confounded the situation by reversing field and advocating the opening of the closed schools, but to this heresy he added building a new school in Crandall and increasing the tax rate further. Parke feared that with Clore's defeat and Coler's wavering vote the West Side would soon have the votes to open the schools and then, satisfied with this victory, turn its back on Crandall, whose children Parke believed had the worst of all educational circumstances in Unit 110.

On the roll-call vote on Kellog's motion to open the schools in Killmer and Tipton, the board split 3-3 (Mrs. Coler being absent), and Kellog's motion to reopen the schools failed. Thus, the battlelines were clearly drawn for the year ahead. Kellog would make motions and negotiate, searching for a way through the web of distrust that had settled over board proceedings, entangling members of the board, on the one hand, and the board and much of the public, on the other. Parke would be the focal point of the West Side's animosity, as he doggedly insisted that he was prepared to compromise and that his vote to open schools would be given in a context of fairness to Crandall and to fiscal responsibility, as he defined it. Perhaps no one on Unit 110's board ever supported more unpopular positions and motions than Fred Parke. Arnold Clore's defeat removed the man that Superintendent Hart thought was the most professional of all the board members. Clore advocated the ultimate consolidation plan—one K–12 school in a centrally located building. Embittered by his defeat, he nonetheless attended most board meetings during the next year, readily overcoming the distress caused by those jubilant West Siders who, on the night of his defeat, wrapped his car in toilet paper, unaware that he was sitting in it at the time.

And immersed in this swirl of plans, motions, referenda, telephone calls, and memorandums, was the very lonely, isolated man at the top, Warren Hart. The board dismisses his recommendations; the board ignores his reactions to the alternatives it has ordered him to explore; the board blames him for its unresolved problems. He sinks lower in the estimation of both East and West Sides as they shift the focal point of their consternation to Hart, to the school board, to Tom Middle (Educational Service Region Board superintendent), or to all three jointly. But it is always Warren Hart who awakes every morning to face—indeed, is paid to face—what seems to be a crowd of crackpots conspiring to keep Unit 110 in the eye of a storm. Crackpots they are not, but they certainly disagree about what to do in Unit 110. At times, they themselves believe they must be crazy to have endured so much confusion for so long.

5

No Resolution in Sight (May 1976–January 1977)

Profound? tragic?—are these fitting terms to characterize Ray Reinhart's feelings about the impact on Killmer of closing its school? And Arnold Clore's feelings about the impact on farmers of maintaining an educational status quo that exacts such a high financial price in educational taxes? I believe they would have us think so. Reinhart is the advocate of cherished community values, whereas Clore is the defender of farmers' well-being, which he sees as tied inextricably to the school district's fiscal health and academic quality. What happens when we juxtapose Clore's and Reinhart's opposing outlooks? The next nine months, May 1976 to January 1977, provide an answer.

These were chaotic months; by portraying them at this distance in time one creates an appearance of patterns and a semblance of order, when neither actually existed. Although new events might "threaten" the stability of the East-West stalemate, such events never caused the stalemated factions to move their discourse to new levels of insight or understanding. The school district suffered as "the bad joke of Illinois"— the place of eternal feuding, the superintendents' graveyard.

An observer of Unit 110 does not always see any better than the insider what its problem is; rather one is often perplexed by the district's capacity for internecine conflict, even impatient with the pig-headedness that seems always to preclude a resolution. The observer, with emotional incapacities rooted elsewhere, wonders why these people can't see the harm they're doing to themselves, why they just can't sit down together, why they fail to grasp the fact that . . . Being locked in combat is as blinding as being in love. This the dispassionate observer should know. In the case of Unit 110, one comes reluctantly to view "locked in combat" as more than a figure of speech—to understand it, on the contrary, as a literal description of the condition of opposing groups who have developed the habit of distrust and the habit of conflict.

The Succession of Events: Overcrowding, Financial Problems, and Secession

As in the period before May 1976, three groups continued to initiate most school district activity: the Killmer Concerned Citizens (KCC), the Citizens Advisory Committee (CAC), and the school board. The efforts of each group twisted around and through the efforts of the other two like twining vines. Joe Kellog, Killmer's board member, was at the center of the board's activities, but given the West Side's view that its board members should represent village and township interests, he also had close contact with the KCC. For the most part, Kellog was not strained by the expectation that he promote Killmer interests. As a Killmer loyalist, he vigorously pursued the opening of Killmer Grade School, searching always for that concept that would shake loose one of the four nay-sayers from his vote and create that narrow but sufficient 4-3 margin to keep the plywood off the windows of his village school. For example, at the May 13 board meeting, after Kucera urged the board to listen to the voters, to make the first conciliatory move to break what he called the "double credibility gap" (neither the voters nor the board trusting one another), Kellog addressed Arlberg with his view of what is reasonable:

Kellog: It's time for that question again, Herb, the one you don't like to hear. It won't hurt if we open the school. We're approaching the point of no return. Killmer is needed in this district; Killmer needs the district. I make a motion we open Killmer and Tipton schools.

Arlberg: My answer's the same as two weeks ago. Till we have more money, I can't reconsider.

Kellog: Do you care if Killmer is in the district?

Arlberg: (He pauses for what seems a long time, too long for Killmer residents to draw any conclusion other than, "He doesn't want us." Then he responds.) I don't know. Lots of things fit into it to say yes or no.

Parke: You ask Arlberg if he wants Killmer in the district, but does Killmer want to stay in?

Kellog: They're meeting tomorrow and that's why I'm asking for a vote tonight. People tell me they'd like to stay in the district, but if they end up with nothing [from the board], they've no alternative but to get out.

Kellog intended to steer the board away from creating a no-hope situation for the KCC, that is, one the KCC would define as no prospect of both staying in Unit 110 and keeping their school open. As the voice of protest and persuasion on the board, he hoped to head off his village's exit, aware that Killmerites discussed it often, and that already flared tempers could easily impel the community to continue to make the choice their own lawyer had advised.

Here, then, was the heart of the issue at this time. The board majority was saying, "Give us the money and we'll open your school," while Killmer was saying, "We have no hope of reopening our school, so we're going to get out." Neither getting out, in the first place, nor getting into the Garrison school district, in the second, would be easy. The former required persuading the seven trustees of the Educational Service Region Board (headed by Superintendent Tom Middle) that secession would not harm Killmer's children educationally, or Unit 110 educationally or financially. The latter proviso, as in past secession cases, required Garrison's accepting Killmer, finding the space for Killmer's high school students (since Killmer would keep its own building as a K–8 school), and receiving Killmer's educational tax revenues the very first year that Killmer joined Garrison. This revenue question involved the "accounting issue,"[1] and it would prove incredibly difficult to resolve. Briefly, it related to whether or not Killmer's detachment from Unit 110 would create a situation that demanded an accounting to take place. If it did, then Killmer would bring its tax revenues to Garrison the first year of its secession; if it did not, Garrison would not receive Killmer's revenues until the second year and Garrison would then have to find some way to finance Killmer's children for one full academic year. With the highest tax rate in Page County, Garrison could not afford to wait one year for Killmer tax money, and thus it was critical to Killmer's plan that an accounting take place in the first year of annexation.

Following Killmer's decision to secede, the CAC explored several proposals and finally developed a plan they hoped would head off both the current financial crisis and Killmer's departure. Their plan was submitted to the board on June 24; its two separate parts embraced, first, retaining a K–6 school in each village (which would please Killmer) and approving a new centralized seventh- and eighth-grade junior high school to be built next to the present high school (which would displease Eaton), and, second, raising $3,000,000 to finance the proposed new junior high school building (which would irritate all tax-paying residents). The board approved this plan 6-1, with Harry Walter of Eaton its lone opponent.

This ostensibly sober CAC discussion and the subsequent school board 6-1 decision had a curious dimension that was perceptible to both groups: what, in fact, was the point of such plans if Killmer left the district? If you have a headache, you seek to remove the cause. Killmer was giving Unit 110 a headache. Syllogistically, Killmer's departure should have been welcome, but here we see otherwise sober men and women devising plans which, by keeping Killmer in the school district, would perpetuate the source of their headache. And here is Joe Kellog, Killmer's representative, supporting these plans at the same time the KCC, composed of his neighbors and friends, and its lawyers prepare to launch a detachment campaign. Indeed, by July 2, 1976, KCC had collected the necessary signatures, filed their petition with Tom Middle of the ESR Board, and learned that the ESR Board would hear its case for detachment at its regular meeting in October.

Though not what one would expect in a season given mostly to fertilizer, flies, and heat, a surreal quality continued to pervade public activity in the summer interim between the old and new academic years. While the CAC worked with an unenthusiastic school board to pass the upcoming referendum scheduled for July 24, the KCC printed and distributed a flier and sample ballot marked with a large X in the NO box. "Blackmail," the flier exclaimed, "that's what the referendum is." The educational tax increase is necessary, the KCC admitted, but the $3,000,000 building plan "if passed, would make it nearly impossible [because of the indebtedness Killmer would assume] for Killmer to detach."

On July 24 KCC energy brought more Killmer voters to the polls than even the larger Eaton and Crandall precincts. District voters overwhelmingly confirmed their opposition both to increasing their educational tax rate (1,216-329) and to building a new junior high school (1,257-283). Only Crandall voters supported both proposals.

"Equal education" was a handy slogan to use in supporting a referendum or a school-board motion, and both sides used it frequently. Parke used it to defend his vote to close schools, on the ground that money saved by consolidation meant money available to support all the children of the district. Parke was particularly disturbed by the fact that East Side children, before they reached high school, had to be bused, while most West Side children of the same age were able to walk to school. Bill Kucera was particularly distressed with Parke's concept of equal education because he thought what Parke really meant was that if education was poor in the East, it was only fair that it be equally poor in the West. At one board meeting, Kucera pressed Parke to clarify his meaning:

Kucera: A question for you, Mr. Parke. Would you please give us your definition of equal education so that it may be written in the minutes of tonight's meeting?

Parke: What purpose is this? What does my definition mean to other board members and other people present tonight?

Kucera: I want to be able to quote you correctly on equal education.

Parke: I must refuse to answer your question. My definition has nothing to do with the working of this board.

Kucera: Mr. Gargan [the board secretary], would you please put Mr. Parke's refusal to answer my question in the minutes of tonight's meeting?

The packed Eaton Grade School, which opened in late August 1976 with students for the first time from both Killmer and Eaton, provided a definite occasion for brandishing the weapon of equal education. Eaton Grade School was undeniably crowded. Though Kellog or Walter might dramatize the facts to suit their purposes, the facts themselves were absolutely self-evident. Kellog established them in an exchange with Carrie Dewack at the board meeting held shortly after Unit 110 opened its doors for the 1976–77 school year. Dewack was not just Eaton's principal; she was an Eaton native, a member of Eaton's village council, and an ardent K–8 supporter.

Kellog: We need to discuss the fifth-grade class of thirty-six kids. We need another classroom and don't have it at Eaton. Is the gym in use every period of day?

Dewack: Far as I can tell right now.

Kellog: The third-grade class is over the gym?

Dewack: Right now they're scheduled to be in it.

Kellog: Gonna have a band on that stage?

Dewack: Yes, couple days per week, first period. P.E. the rest of the week.

Kellog: Don't that room have kids wall to wall up there? Can't get by the desks?
Dewack: Yes.
Kellog: Fourth grade is another problem. Fourteen in one class?
Dewack: Twenty-three in the other class. Thirty-seven is the total.
Kellog: Not quite equal education is it?

Kellog moved to reopen Killmer's school. The motion failed, of course, by a 4-3 vote.

Equal education was a rhetorical smoke screen that could distract attention only momentarily from more heartfelt concerns. The board simultaneously battled over developing suitable means to relieve Eaton's overcrowding and to manage its continually escalating financial problem. Hart, ineffectual but nevertheless responsible, summoned his five principals to discuss Eaton's overcrowding. The connection between overcrowding and finances was clear to Hart. After noting the litter generated by ten years of defeated referenda, Hart drew this moral: Don't try to centralize; give Killmer what it wants or "we're not gonna get a damn dime." Joe Kellog, also present for this meeting, demonstrated his capacity to compromise by agreeing to leave the West Side's seventh- and eighth-graders in a centralized junior high school as a price to pay for an open K–6 in Killmer, no small concession considering his commitment to the K–8 rationale. "My personal opinion," he said, "is that the issue is not East against West. It is people in the district holding on to something. We need to come up with a workable plan if we're going to get the money from the people."

Kellog's comment here is truly perceptive. The heart of the conflict in Unit 110 is the persistent desire of people to hold on to something. Regrettably, the different groups did not want to hold on to the same things; they did not necessarily see as legitimate what the other group desired; and, as the situation was defined, one group's satisfaction entailed the other group's loss. To that extent, Kellog was mistaken: East and West did oppose each other.

It was a useful meeting; the administrators clearly recognized the gravity of the responsibility they shared with Hart and responded accordingly. They worked in a districtwide spirit, aware of the East-West rivalry and Killmer's determination to detach. Undeterred by their possibly impending fragmentation, they conceived the following plan, which Hart presented to the board in mid-September: (1) open a K–3 in Tipton (their 4–6 students would attend Oldham's school), a K–6 in the other four villages, and continue the centralized junior high in Crandall; (2) hold a referendum on October 30 to increase tax revenues; and (3) employ a financial consultant to advise Hart on selling cash flow bonds.

On this mid-September occasion, the board was in a particularly pertinacious mood. Of the three proposals the administrative group developed, the board accepted only one—the employment of the financial consultant—and refused even to vote on the other two. To almost everyone's surprise, it also refused to approve a budget for the 1976–77 school year. Of course, the board must approve some budget some time because, for example, it must pay teachers' and bus drivers' salaries, buy supplies, etc., but its disapproval is a measure of the frustration of the board members (Parke, Kellog, Kucera, and Walter) who refused to face this unavoidable reality. These four expressed their sense of desperation at the intractable perplexities of Unit 110 by rejecting the budget. Superintendent Hart expressed his desperation to the board and assembled onlookers at this same mid-September meeting:

> I tried to bring Unit 110 together, not to let it be two, as it appears to be now. We need to look at some history of past referenda. The people have not only said "No," they've said "Hell no." We haven't done a good PR job. We've forgotten about the kids, the purpose that we're sitting here. I have, I admit it. Unit 110 has had problems for many years and I don't see any clear solution.

To be sure, at a later meeting a budget was finally approved, but exchanges between Kellog and Kucera and Parke and Arlberg became more heated and accusatory, especially as the school district's financial picture finally became unequivocably clear.

Superintendent Hart's estimates of the seriousness of the district's financial problems were often called in doubt by school-board members and by school-district residents, depending on whether his estimates supported or undermined their points of view. Uncertain of the facts, people did not know how concerned they should be. The financial consultants the school board hired confirmed that the district's expenses exceeded its income and that its debt was mounting at the rate of $200,000 each year. With doubt of its financial problem now laid to rest, board members and residents could agree that Unit 110 faced: (1) the prospect of Killmer Township's imminent secession; (2) probable loss of state aid (for failing to complete work required to maintain the safety of district buildings); and (3) possible bankruptcy. In the minds of many, this triptych of bad news even dampened the euphoria of the high school's winning football season. (Under the circumstances, the fact of a football season is a heartening reminder that Unit 110 is an arena for school activities as well as for disputes.)

The Educational Service Region Board provided a brief diversion from this drama and a bit of hope for those who wished to see Unit 110 kept intact. (For some of those the wish was sentimental, but for most it was purely financial, since Killmer's departure from Unit 110 would further strain its diminishing budget.) At its October 19, 1976, meeting, the ESR Board dismissed the KCC detachment petition on the grounds of a technicality brought to its attention by Harold Parker, a Killmer township landowner and lawyer who opposed Killmer's detachment.

Reinhart responded to the board's rejection of his group's petition with an ominous assessment of sentiment in Killmer: "I think people believe the only hope is to get out of Unit 110 even if the school is opened." Until this time, the general feeling in Killmer and the rest of Unit 110 was that an open school in Killmer would terminate Killmer's secession campaign. Reinhart's statement foreshadowed an escalation of tension in the school district and the entry of Unit 110's conflict upon a new phase.

Notwithstanding Reinhart's comment, Killmer residents were torn by needing to take action in two conflicting directions, one on behalf of their dream of secession, the other on behalf of their despair of remaining in Unit 110. In regard to the latter, they decided that if and when the CAC recommended and the board accepted another tax-increase referendum, they would support it. This paradoxical decision simply points up the ambivalence among KCC members about steering a course in total disregard of the school district's welfare. They also were mindful of the potential influence of "having done the right thing" on the decision of whatever body would determine the outcome of their detachment petition.

Their judgment would soon be tested. Given the CAC's belief that the district faced financial ruin, the CAC urged the board to arrange a tax-increase referendum before December 30, 1976, and also to reorganize. Mrs. Coler moved that the board postpone its response to this proposal and study its details at a special study session. Though she had no alternatives of her own to offer, she was distressed by the CAC's recommendation of only a K–3 in her village (Tipton) in contrast to a K–6 in the other four. She was to remain at the center of board activity for the next few weeks.

November 30, 1976, was the date of Mrs. Coler's suggested special study session. Hart, with the board's concurrence, invited Tom Middle to attend because he, as the state's educational agent in Page County, was responsible for ensuring the safety of the county's buildings (which like all public school buildings are state property). Middle went straight to the point. He warned the board that life-safety work at Eaton must be done; that if it were not done, Unit 110 could lose its state aid; and that the state would take over the district if it could not or would not pay its bills. With the state's position now clear, the board moved directly to the CAC proposals:

Kellog: Well, to me it looks as if a referendum is our last real chance to get added revenue in our next tax collection. We're gonna have to get more money.

Hart: No matter what Killmer does, we've got to have more money to operate.

Parke: What's your pleasure, board?

Kucera: I'd like to make a motion that the Killmer and Tipton schools be open in time for the students when they return from vacation on January 3.

Walter: I'll second.

Coler: I'm just going to say I'm going to support this. It's the only way we're ever going to get any increase in taxes.

Parke restated the motion and the secretary called the roll and recorded the responses. Mrs. Coler broke ranks. She joined the West Side trio to provide the necessary 4-3 majority. Hart had indicated that he could complete the required shift of the district's elementary children over the Christmas vacation. With this assurance, Mrs. Coler yielded to the pressure for a resolution of problems that had gripped all board members for so many months. When the meeting was over, the large group in attendance did not depart, as it did from all other board meetings, amidst its usual murmurrings. Mrs. Coler's about-face had made this a memorable occasion. Those present filed out of the boardroom and congregated in the adjacent office; there was no reason to stay, but they were too dazed and happy to leave.

Within one week of Mrs. Coler's apostasy, the board met for its next regular meeting. By this time, all board members had become disturbed by their recent decision. Even Joe Kellog acknowledged that the board had behaved precipitously and thus urged his colleagues to rescind their 4-3 vote to open schools now and to "do our homework to get started for next year." However, his suggestion was meant only for those parts of the proposal pertaining to Tipton and the East Side. With great emotion he said, "You don't have to move East Side kids, but we need to in Eaton or the kids can get hurt."

More surprises were in store at this meeting. A man in the audience, a Tipton resident and pastor of a local church there, requested and received permission to speak. Then, with the consent of the board president, he gave the board copies of a petition signed by 994 persons from Crandall, Oldham, and

Tipton; these signatures had been collected in less than one week. The point of the petition, the petition spokesman said, is that we do not want the schools to be reopened on January 3. We want them open, but in September, not in January. This degree of mobilization on the East Side was unprecedented in Unit 110's history. Following this dramatic act of East Side will, Gargan made a motion to reclose Tipton and Killmer's schools and it passed with a 4-3 vote. Mrs. Coler, whose telephone had rung a great deal in the previous week, was back in rank, and Killmer's jubilation had proved painfully ephemeral.

The board rejected the midyear opening of Killmer and Tipton schools, but it did not reject holding the referenda it had earlier approved. Accordingly, Superintendent Hart made the necessary arrangements, and Unit 110 residents went to the polls on December 18 to determine whether or not to increase their assessed valuation. Only Killmer, mobilized by its KCC, approved. No one took hope from the fact that the referenda were defeated by a significantly narrower margin than the ones held in June 1976 to surmise that a new, positive spirit might be emerging in the district.

As 1976 ended, all CAC recommendations had been rejected, all Joe Kellog's efforts to relieve overcrowding in Eaton by reopening Killmer Grade School had failed, no life-safety work had been done, Garrison residents and school board wavered in their acceptance of a merger with Killmer, and KCC spirits sagged as they awaited the January 25, 1977, hearing on their detachment petition:

Member: The flier we [KCC] sent out about donating money was taken wrong by many people. Some assumed that it was almost pushing them into donating. The school is not the most important thing on their minds anymore. People are getting used to not having a school in town.

Member: You can't keep up this momentum forever. Most of the people I talked to feel if this one [the ESR Board hearing of their petition] doesn't go through, then we should drop

it. Middle told someone that he wouldn't want his kid in
Unit 110.''
Member: After we've gone so far and done so much you hate
to say we'll just give up, but . . .

Perspectives on the Events:
Four School Board Members

At this point a pause in the narrative to let four responsible
residents speak in their own voices about the continuing crisis
may help to demonstrate how Unit 110's conflict derives from
varying interpretations of what is at stake when a school closes
and how appropriate it is to close schools as a means of re-
solving financial problems. Their words may show, too, how
complex are the strands of thought, motive, explanation, and
activity which run through this unhappy struggle.

Bill Kucera, Eaton, teaches junior high school math in
Pageville. Herb Arlberg, Crandall countryside, farms on land
that his family has owned for over one hundred years. Harry
Walter, Eaton, is an electrician. Sarah Coler, Tipton countryside, is a landowner and farmer's wife. All are Unit 110 board
members and, in their own fashion, all are concerned about
what happens in their school district. Only Kucera is not a
native of the area, and only he is married to someone who did
not grow up in the area. Each of these four board members
has a perspective which illuminates Unit 110's conflict (the first
three were speaking in the late fall or early winter of 1976;
Mrs. Coler was speaking in February 1977).

Bill Kucera, Eaton
"I'll tell you why I resist consolidation. Bigger is better?
It's not true. You lose your identity and become a number;
you're treated like cattle, not human beings. If you stand at
my classroom door [in Pageville] you see a school of a thousand
junior high kids. We have fights, extortion, and brutality every
day. In a small school it's easy to control; it's there but easy
to suppress. If it rears its head, it gets clobbered. Here, where
anonymity is rife, kids can do things and get away with it.

Also, Killmer students don't belong in Eaton; they're inter-
lopers in Eaton. And why bus when you don't have to, when
a kid can be home? I don't want my kids to get a sex education
on the bus.

"The issue is not what is the best plan for education. The
issue is to keep the buildings open in Killmer, Eaton, and Tipton. It's not whether you get a better education in a larger or
smaller district. It's pro and con both ways. It's a personal
preference whether you go to a large or small attendence center; it's as simple as that. It's my belief that parents should
have the ultimate say so in how their children are educated,
and I will fight for that. Now if Killmer wants out, I feel they
should go. As far as the district is concerned, no, they should
not go. They're going to hurt the district financially when they
take out their students. Their 350 kids are spread nice and even
throughout the whole system so you chop down very few staff
members if those kids leave.

"As a board member I don't get any pressure; strangely
enough, everybody leaves me alone. I know, I think I know,
how Eaton wants me to vote, and nobody in Eaton ever threat-
ens me. I vote the way I want; it's also the way Eaton wants.
It's just a happy coincidence that it comes out that way."

Killmer, on the contrary, is not blessed with a "happy
coincidence" or good fortune of any sort which augurs well for
its future. By the time of these interviews, the village's repu-
tation was the unenviable one of, "Can't live with 'em and
can't live without 'em." For example, Kucera invariably sup-
ports the reopening of Killmer's school, but opposes their
secession. Coler does not deny comments she has heard to the
effect that as long as Killmer remains in the school district, the
district will always face contention. And Arlberg, as we learn
below, thinks Unit 110 would benefit by Killmer's departure
to Garrison, but he, like Kucera, endorses the involvement of
the district's lawyer to oppose Killmer in its secession hearing.

Herbert Arlberg, Crandall Countryside
"We've operated from one crisis to the next ever since
I've been on the board. I've always wanted a five-year edu-
cational plan, but something always comes up. We made the

present plan to close Killmer and Tipton, and we were determined not to change it, but we've had no cooperation to make it work. Citizens throw monkey wrenches in our plans so they can't work. We've never been threatened with lawsuits before. I believe our attorney should attend all meetings to keep us from going off the deep end, to prevent us from doing something illegal. If I knew that suit they threatened [in the 1975 tape-measure victory for the West Side, which kept their children out of the proposed centralized junior high school in Crandall] wouldn't have had any significance, that the state wouldn't have cracked the whip at us, . . . if that junior high plan would have worked, we wouldn't have had to make the drastic moves this year [1976] in Eaton. We were led to believe there'd be savings from the loss of teachers and not so much extra cost in transportation, but we've had an increase in enrollment and this [because of the teacher's contract] requires teacher aides. Hart didn't recommend this move, but he maintained it would save money. It hasn't; at least as of now it hasn't. From the board's standpoint, the closing was sound. If we had the cooperation we hoped for in Eaton, it might've worked out. But they're saying Eaton's too crowded to have good education.

"Nobody on the board makes a decision out of spite. They do what they think is best. I'm sorry that the issues have got people so upset because since I'll never move, I'll be seeing people who'll be angry with me for the rest of my life."

There is a good measure of wishful thinking in Arlberg's expectation of cooperation from Eaton. Nobody alert and alive in Unit 110 since Gaumnitz's failed effort to build a central junior high school could believe that Eaton would passively accept an overcrowded K–6 school and the loss of its seventh- and eighth-graders. Although he will consistently reject Kellog's motions to reopen Killmer Grade School, he reveals his regret about the way things turned out. It takes a more single-minded Clore or Parke to be impervious to the controlling reality of small towns and small school districts. Arlberg sadly points out—"I'll be seeing people who'll be angry with me the rest of my life."

"I feel I have a dual purpose on the board. I've always stated kids should come first, but we seven board members actually represent the taxpayers. The superintendent and one hundred teachers and administrators fight for the course of studies; as far as saying, 'Let's be financially responsible to the taxpayers,' that's the seven members. I hope my views are tempered by. thoughts of children, but I want to be fair to taxpayers. Not many people come to board meetings to say hold expenses down.

"The West Side—they're against anything that might help the East Side of the district, afraid of some advantage coming here. Probably the best thing is for Killmer to go to Garrison. This will create money problems, but we can deal with them if there's not so much distress and dissension and distrust. With Killmer gone, we could sit down, after soul searching, PR, and selling, and we could work out a solution.

"The point now is, do we do what's best in terms of money or to end the controversy? It's hard to figure out. If we do what is educationally and financially sound, I'm condemned for thinking in money terms, but if everyone gets what they want and we don't have the money to operate, what can be done?"

Like Clore and many other farmers, Arlberg is not strongly attached to any village. We identify him as being from the Crandall countryside—in fact, he lives quite close to Crandall—but his farm and home are in Crawford Township, which does not contain a single village. And he was bused all the years he went to school. So neither the business nor the community-decline arguments against consolidation strike a personal chord. Yet, he reacts as though he comprehends the concerns which underlie these arguments. In the end, he identifies his overriding rationale for consolidation as a commitment to the taxpayer. As he states his case, it is not just his personal commitment, it is his duty to stress financial considerations. Of course, he, like everyone else associated with schools, emphasizes that "kids come first." After a while, one becomes callous about such an assertion, suspecting that it is one that must be made first before the speaker can state what comes second (and what, in truth, he or she feels most strongly about).

Harry Walter, Eaton

Harry Walter, lifelong resident of Eaton, is a taciturn man in public. Any time he speaks, however, it is straightforward. He does not entangle himself in the tortuous contingencies of school finance and organization in Unit 110. He is full of opinions and he never fails to vote on any board motion that deals with these issues, but it is one article of faith that dominates his concern—the maintenance of a K–8 school in Eaton. Because of this, he is dedicated to helping Killmer maintain its K–8 school. Walter has no sympathy for "the taxpayers," that general group identified by Arlberg but which for him clearly refers to the farmers. Walter's commitment is to Eaton. Period. He can't talk about Unit 110 without going back to its beginning. His thoughts turn from perceptions of conspiracy to hard fact.

"It's been our thought that way back in 1947 the plan started to get the schools of these five towns consolidated in Crandall. Now, we have a firm belief in this. They've never let up since then; we haven't either. And we're not going to. We thought that we had done them quite a favor when we let them build the high school there in Crandall. The only way it happened was to bring our K–8s back home, which they did, and so we didn't mind. Ever since they got the high school, they've been working on the grade schools. As much time as I've put in on it, I really can't pinpoint any one individual rounding this up in Crandall. Thomas Stoughton, I'd always thought that Tom was the ringleader. Tom died and it still continues. There's got to be somebody spearheading it over there somewhere. Doesn't make any difference what superintendent we have; doesn't make any difference what board members we have. It's still there, somebody continually wanting centralization of these five towns in Crandall. I hear it, I see it on the school board—somebody is always proposing consolidation. I think they want the whole thing just for the sake of having it in Crandall; yes, not for educational reasons, for Crandall reasons.

"Our K–8 group used to meet every Monday night faithfully, probably for at least four years. I was the chairman. Had a turnout average of ten people, unless we had an election or something coming up. We started just harassing the board every time they had a meeting. We would set and think of things to make them ponder before they could answer them. We'd do our homework and we'd get the answer. Hell, I knew more about the board when I wasn't on it than I do now.

"We had enough talent between us that we made up a plan of our own that would put a K–8 school in every community. It was for less than a million-and-a-half dollars, instead of the board's three million dollars. That's all they ever know, is three million dollars. [He laughs.] You'd think that that was a limit. We got ourselves on the board agenda and my nephew and I presented our plan. We spent about an hour going through our slides and answering questions. After we were through and sat back down in the audience, Mr. Talman says to someone, 'Well, you can't let a bunch of dumb shits come over and tell you how to run your school.' Well, that made us furious. From then on we dropped all course of trying to work with them. Our next thing was to get rid of Mr. Talman, which we proceeded to do, and succeeded, incidentally. We put Fred Parke on the board. We thought he was what we needed to straighten things up a little bit. He was just as stubborn about a junior high as I am about a K–8. We gave Parke and Gargan the boost, you might say. So then along comes Mr. Arlberg to our meetings. And he swore before God and everybody that he wanted a school in each town. Three days before the election we got the rumor that he wasn't on our side, that he was just pulling our leg. We had time for a write-in, but we were afraid to take that chance because we needed that seat on the board very badly. Far as I know, from that day to this day, he's never had not one, not one little teensy bit of a kind word for Eaton, Killmer, or anybody over here. It's all been consolidation. And jab you if you can.

"I talked to Hart the first night he happened to be super-intendent; had a meeting with him at his request, not mine. I wasn't on the school board then. I take it that in his interviews he'd been informed of K–8. I didn't beat around the bush: I said, 'We're going to be here twice as long after you're gone if you mess up what we've got.' And he says, 'I want to tell you, Mr. Walter, that I'm not coming over to rock the boat or to make waves.' And I said, 'That's good, 'cause if you do, you're going down the drain.'

"Mr. Hart has got himself in hot water. There've been things that have come before that board that they had no more business being there than flying backwards. It's like the school calendar. He'll bring up the school calendar at a meeting and say, 'Well, now, this is what the teachers want.' Nine times out of ten the board will vote and accept it. Next thing you run into four or five teachers and they say, 'Jesus Christ, what kind of a calendar have we got this year?' 'It's what the teachers want.' 'Who? At the meeting we had there was no teacher that wanted it.' Well, you know, once in a while you can take a complaint like this and throw it to the wind. But you can't take complaints like this all the time. I hear them continually.

"We've never given up hope. This is the first year that we went down the drain that I can remember. Eaton and Killmer has always raised enough hell, that's the only thing that you could say, they raised enough hell that they got what they wanted. Well, it's been our belief that if we didn't like what they done, we went and told them. Until this year Eaton and Killmer has always voiced their opinions very strongly and we've usually, not always, come out with keeping our school. Catching hell all year, yes, but we were able to keep the school. Now I don't think they'll get the money in the referendum [December 21, 1976]. I will not recommend anybody to vote for it, and I'll be asked many, many times. I would have voted for it had they opened the schools. I think they stood a chance if they'd sent the kids back home. I don't think they stand a chance now. The board cannot be trusted. It's a very nervous board. How they sleep at night, I'll never know. They get more or less harassed in every direction."

Unit 110 residents often remark that they would never be a school board member. They realize that what Harry Walter, the former self-professed harasser of board members, says is true: "They get more or less harassed in every direction." Thankless, unpaid jobs do not attract long lines of people waiting to fill them. Walter had been an antagonist of the school for so long that even now, when he is a board member, he refers to the board as "they." It is probably only in reference to Eaton that he would say "we." From such partisans, compromises do not readily emerge.

Sarah Coler, Tipton Countryside

Sarah Coler recalls why she agreed to run for the board
in the first place. Increasingly, she wonders about the wisdom
of her decision, as she is caught in the cross fire between
conflicting factions, each appealing to her strained conscience,
on the one hand, to be responsive to financial considerations,
and, on the other, to preserve community schools.

"I had no intention of running for the board, but then,
when I thought about it, I really kind of enjoyed the idea 'cause
I hadn't done anything for so long. I was thinking that it would
give me something to do to use my head for something other
than what I was going to fix for the next meal. I enjoyed it until
we started fighting so much; I don't like that. The fighting—I
think it was the lack of money. For a while, they talked about
closing only the Tipton school. Then one thing led to another
and they finally agreed to close the two, one here and one at
Killmer, 'cause I think they realized that was the only way they
could get anything done.

"Tipton's reaction to their school being closed this year?
Oh, some of them just hate it, but not to the point they're going
to fight it like Killmer. Killmer tried to get them to go in with
them, and they wouldn't do it. The only reason, now this is
strictly my reason, is because most of them that are in Tipton
lived there all their lives and they knew that every so many
years they go through this [the board shifting children from
one school to another], and I think they thought that there
wasn't any point in wasting money going to court. There's just
never been harmony in this unit. I've heard some people say,
'Well, as long as we have Killmer, there'll be fighting.' My
husband went to school here years back and said he could
remember his dad fighting. . . .

"Most of the ones on the West Side that are on that committee [KCC] fighting us are not people that have always lived
in Killmer. I'll bet the longest ones haven't lived there over
ten or twelve years. They've moved out of Pageville trying to
get away from conditions there. I think they think they have
a good thing in Killmer and they want to keep it. Their school
is right there [in town]. If you move out to get into that [the
"good thing" of Killmer] and then all of a sudden it's taken
away from you . . . Well, the people I talked to in Killmer all

own land and they don't feel that way, but they figure you can get ostracized pretty easy in these little towns, so they wouldn't go against what the KCC supported. You know, when that committee comes around with a petition, the farmers sign it, but they say they really don't feel that way about it. This is what they tell me. That's part of small-town living, really. I still don't think they have the right to come in [and tell us what to do] when we're the ones that are really paying the bulk of it—the farm people. An awful lot of people in Browne Township,[2] like my own relatives, own a lot of land there. See, they pay taxes year after year and they are high.''

Mrs. Coler is even more candid than Arlberg in exposing her obligation to landowners. To her and to others the logic is clear: if you are ''paying the bulk of it,'' then you acquire rights which should be given preeminence in policy decisions. However, like Arlberg, she is aware of countervailing considerations, such as the ''good thing'' Killmerites do not want to relinquish.

''I don't know, I guess I'm kind of wishy-washy. I feel guilty that I'm letting down some of the board members because they feel so strongly about consolidation. But I don't care if it's the school or whatever, regardless of what my opinion was, I wouldn't feel it was so much better that I'd force it on somebody if they didn't think that way. If Killmer wants to have their little school, why, I'll probably try and help them get it. Really, I probably shouldn't look at it this way at all, but if it's just for saving us money [the school closings], should money be the basis for the decision? Well, no, probably the education and the welfare of the children should be the first thing.

''One thing that bothers me terribly is that just on the spur of the moment they'll be talking about consolidating or something, and then, all of a sudden, one of them will make a motion to close such and such a school or open such and such a school. And they really don't have that much discussion on it. You have to make up your mind just like that and I don't like to make that fast a decision. There's been many a time I really didn't think they gave [the motion] enough thought. After going to those meetings for a while I eventually didn't get sick to my stomach because you knew a motion was coming.

"Right before Christmas vacation the advisory council [CAC] had come up with a recommendation to open both schools [Killmer and Tipton] and to run this referendum. One of the men changed this and said to open them right when the kids came back from Christmas vacation. I went along with it. That was another one that just came up bing-bang, have a motion. So before I voted I asked Mr. Hart, 'Is there anything or any reason that this couldn't be done at that time?' And he said, 'No, nothing that I know of.' Well, what I meant was would they have time during Christmas vacation to get all the work done that this move involved. No, he couldn't think of any reason why not. And boy, after I got home and thought about it, I was so angry with him, because the students had never had their semester exams yet. All right, they were going to be changing schools in about ten days and they'd have to take semester exams from a different teacher with different classmates. It was terrible, I'll tell you; my phone never stopped ringing. Starting the next day after the board meeting it rang constantly. People did not want their school open after Christmas. They wanted the school open, but not until the next school year. When I went to the next meeting [December 3, 1976], I still didn't know for sure what I was going to do. But I knew it was coming up that they were going to make a motion to open the buildings. When I got to the meeting there were a bunch of Tipton people with the petitions nine hundred people had signed, so I did rescind my position. I came home and I told Ben [her husband], I said, 'Well, when you see the paper I'll look like the village idiot.' For a while it seemed like every time I went there I was changing my mind."

Despite her fundamental concern for the landowner, Mrs. Coler is the only board member who does not reflexively take a position either for or against consolidation. Consequently, when, as she indicated, a motion to reopen schools suddenly was placed before the board, she would feel bewildered by the pace of a discussion that did not leave matters sufficiently clarified for her. I believe she truly did not want to force the West Side to accept decisions they so strenuously resisted.

However, when motions came to be voted upon, it was almost always the landowner's position that determined her decision.

One must marvel at the various facets of this prolonged educational melodrama. Will Killmer be allowed to secede? If allowed, can Garrison afford to absorb Killmer's students? Can the Citizen's Advisory Committee devise a plan that will prove acceptable to the Killmer Concerned Citizens and to the school board's proconsolidation majority? Can Superintendent Hart establish the credibility and exert the leadership necessary to break the deadlock between school board members seemingly frozen into adversary roles? Will the usually lethargic East Side residents refuse to tolerate the West Side's agitation and use their voter majority to reorganize Unit 110 to their satisfaction? And so on.

By January 1977, on the eve of a snowfall so deep that some rural families would be homebound for a week by ten-foot drifts, weary school-district residents had no reason to think that relief was imminent. The past year's events had taken the form of a grade C film whose producers, failing to find a way to culminate the action, persist in shooting the same spluttering scene over and over, hinting at a finale that never comes. In this scene, the cameras zoom in close as the school board session is gaveled to order; the routine business items on the agenda are quickly dispensed with. Just as Mrs. Coler seems about to relax, we hear a motion and a second to reopen Killmer's and Tipton's grade schools, followed by a blur of discussion. Then Mrs. Coler, now quite unrelaxed, adds her nay to a three-three tie to defeat the motion. This scene is replayed, ad infinitum.

But, if the KCC and its supporters grow weary and despairing, they still keep alive the hope that their detachment petition will get a positive reception from the trustees of the Educational Service Region. Barring this, they can once again change the arena of their struggle to the forthcoming April school board election when Gargan and Arlberg, part of the "nay" majority, come up for election.

6

Petitions, Politics, and Perturbations:
January to September, 1977

The Secession Hearing: Petitions

January 25, 1977, was an auspicious day for Killmer and Unit 110—it was the long-awaited occasion when the Educational Service Region Board would hear its detachment case. The KCC had once again obtained the necessary signatures of two-thirds of all legal Killmer Township voters on petitions to withdraw from the district, just as it had last fall in preparation for the October 19, 1976, hearing when the ESR Board dismissed Killmer's petition. The dismissal in October spurred the KCC to obtain even more signatures than it had the first time. One very old woman who spilled some cherry juice on the petition that had been brought to her to sign said she'd sign it in blood if it would keep the school in Killmer. For persons of all ages in Killmer Township, detachment had become that sort of an issue.

The late *Killmer News* editor Glenn Davids would have been pleased this 25th day of January; were he still alive, he certainly would have been among those relative few who crowded into the ESR Board room where Superintendent Tom Middle presided. The room contained about eighty chairs and every one was occupied, though many more Killmer supporters would have flocked to the hearing had not the KCC advised them to stay home. At the meeting-room door, an ESR Board employee asked all entrants if they wished to provide testimony and, like at a wedding with places marked off for the bride's and the groom's relatives and friends, he ascertained which side of the case their testimony would support and seated them accordingly. At 9:15 A.M., with the audience, advocates, reporters, and court stenographers in place, the lawyers (Bill Stoughton for Unit 110 and Farris Herbst for the KCC) prepared to call their witnesses.

Tom Middle and his trustees were arrayed in a long line across the front of the room, the court stenographer and her machine clicking away to their right, the board lawyer and his witnesses placed to their left. Both lawyers would be citing school law found in the *School Code of Illinois* in a section called "Boundary Change—New District" (State of Illinois 1969). Only two parts of this section were directly applicable to the case of Killmer's desired detachment from Unit 110 and annexation to the existing Garrison School District:

> 1. The Hearing Board shall hear the petition and determine the sufficiency thereof and may adjourn the hearing from time to time or continue the matter for want of sufficient notice or for other good cause. The Hearing Board *(a)* shall hear evidence as to the school needs and conditions of the territory in the area within and adjacent thereto, and as to the ability of the districts affected to meet the standards of recognition as prescribed by the Superintendent of Public Instruction, *(b)* shall take into consideration the division of funds and assets which will result from any change of boundaries, and the will of the people of the area affected, and *(c)* shall determine whether it is to the best interests of the schools of the area and the educational welfare of the pupils should such change in boundaries be granted. [54]

> 2. Whenever a part of a district is included within the boundaries of a newly created district the county board of school trustees shall cause an accounting to be had between the districts affected by the change in boundaries as pro-

vided in Sections 7-16 to 7-26 of this Act, each inclusive; however, there shall be no accounting made after a mere change in boundaries when no new district is created. [62]

The first part above covers assurances and circumstances that KCC lawyer Farris Herbst would have to establish for Killmer's case to be upheld; the second, the previously referred to "accounting issue," would be a matter of judgment and interpretation, beyond the scope of the ESR Board of Trustees and thus requiring a ruling from the state's legal staff. The KCC would strive to verify that the removal of an entire township to a different school district surely occasioned more than a "mere change in boundaries," even though "no new district is created."

Reinhart was the first of ten witnesses Herbst questioned as part of the KCC's orchestrated plan to document their case. Several of this group's presentations had moments suffused with feeling, but for the most part they were straightforward statements of corroboration designed to win the day on the strength of their factual rather than of their emotional appeal. Reinhart and his colleagues truly believed they had a verifiable case, though they were not assured that it would be accepted as such by the ESR Board trustees.

To begin, Reinhart traced the origin of the Killmer Concerned Citizens group and the recent history of Unit 110. He clarified that because the board refused to consider increasing the educational tax rate, a prerequisite to opening Killmer's school, the KCC was left with the choices of staying in Unit 110 to "fight and fight and fight," as they had done since the district was formed, or seeking the peace and opportunity promised by annexation to Garrison.

Nancy Franklin, Ned Ruback, and Elliot Argyle followed with a general picture of the extensive busing currently required to transport Killmer's children to schools in Eaton and Crandall, compared to the significantly reduced busing possible if they joined Garrison; and with the specific picture of unpleasantness parents faced in sending their elementary children to Eaton and junior high children to Crandall—early awakenings, rushed breakfasts, extended waits for buses to arrive, and long bus rides. Ruback estimated that his fifth-grader, bused to Eaton, was gone from home for eight hours each school day, but only five of those hours were spent in her classroom; he was no less distressed that his daughter now attended school with "strangers":

> My daughter was asked to a birthday and slumber party at Eaton. I am a concerned parent. I like to know where she is, who she's with. I did not know the people that invited her. . . . My wife and I could not give an answer and more or less had to investigate who she was going to be with, which created somewhat of a problem.

To complete the morning session, Herbst called Mary Reeder, Killmer newcomer and energetic participant on the KCC executive committee. She and her husband Alf Reeder, a Pageville College professor, are political activists who got wind of the school-closing issue in Killmer soon after moving to their old farmhouse. They thought the issue merited involvement, although their only child was two years away from attending school. Mary Reeder's testimony addressed two critical points in regard to the school code's requirements for successful detachment—curriculum and financial impact. Having made an exhaustive comparative analysis of the curricular offerings of Unit 110 and the Garrison School District, she concluded that not only would Killmer children not suffer from a move to Garrison, they would benefit from it in all grades, K through 12. She summarized her curricular findings by presenting each district's relative expenditures per student. Overall, Garrison budgeted $1,558.00 per pupil and Unit 110 $1,312.00, with per-pupil expenditures for supplies, textbooks, equipment, and the library ranging from 20 to 300 percent more in Garrison. Reeder matched this felicitous comparative picture with what to her were less than dismal financial implications for Unit 110. If Killmer detached, Unit 110 would suffer a loss, since that township's property produced about $300,000 in tax revenue and its students accounted for expenses of about $207,000. She estimated, however, that Unit 110, with Page

County's lowest tax rate, could readily compensate for this loss of $93,000 by a 28¢/$100 tax increase. Also on the plus side for Unit 110, Killmer's departure would eliminate all space problems in the schools Killmer children now attend. Reeder's arguments and data were calculated to reassure the trustees that the "best interests" and "educational welfare" of pupils affected by detachment would not be in jeopardy.

The morning was devoted entirely to the KCC side; most of the afternoon session was split equally between witnesses for detachment and witnesses Bill Stoughton called in behalf of Unit 110. Before turning over the floor to Stoughton, Herbst called several more witnesses, closing his case with Killmer village board member Roger Corcoran who attested to the village's need of a school to assure its vitality and continued growth.

Corcoran spoke for a minute at most, but it was already mid-afternoon and some of the older ESR Board trustees were fighting heavy eyelids. Bill Stoughton mercifully called only five witnesses, beginning with Superintendent Warren Hart. By this time in his tenure as district superintendent, Hart had become more familiar than he cared to be with judicial and quasi-judicial proceedings. Weary and fed up as he was with the protracted, seemingly insoluble disorder of his school district, Hart nonetheless responded forthrightly to Stoughton's probes, explaining that the board closed Killmer's school because of the school district's financial problems; that life-safety work remained undone at both Eaton's and Killmer's grade schools; that the curriculum of Unit 110 was not substandard compared to Garrison's; and that the effect on Unit 110 of Killmer's detaching would be negative. Stoughton intended Hart's testimony to counteract the effect of Mary Reeder's and others' which suggested that there existed a firm curricular and financial basis for the detachment case. But the strongest and longest rebuttal of the entire KCC case came from Charles Thornton, lawyer and landowner in the eastern section of Killmer Township, and the man responsible for establishing the specific point upon which Killmer's petition foundered in its October effort. Thornton did not attack either the community school concept or Garrison; he said he preferred to stay in Unit 110. Why, Thornton argued, should Killmer be allowed to disrupt Unit 110? Moreover, he continued, if Killmer becomes unhappy in Garrison, then it may seek one place after the other, in what could become a perpetual quest for a security which should be sought in the political and not in the judicial arena. In short, change the school board, he urged.

Following several more witnesses, a recess, and each lawyer's summation of the arguments for his side, Jack Bone, Garrison's attorney, then made the last major presentation of consequence before the 4:15 P.M. adjournment. Bone said that the Garrison school board, after examining the pros and cons of Killmer's detachment and annexation to Garrison, agreed that to avoid injuring its own students, Killmer had to bring to Garrison (1) its grade school and equipment, (2) the revenue from all of the township's rural areas (notably from Charles Thornton and his neighbors, who threatened to secede from Killmer Township if Killmer seceded from Unit 110), and (3) all of its educational tax revenues in the first year Killmer joined Garrison (the accounting issue, again).

Thus ended about six hours of advocacy, a long, taxing day for all concerned, and a fascinating one for those who were interested in the issue but had no personal stake in its outcome.

The KCC reached a high point in its organizational activity with its detachment preparations for the ESR Board hearing. Uncertain when the ESR Board would report its findings, however, and uncertain what those findings would be, the KCC had to decide whether or not to proceed as though it might have to remain in Unit 110. Depending on its decision, it faced the anomaly of arduously preparing for the forthcoming school board election in April, while hoping desperately that as of the next academic year, 1977–78, Killmer would be annexed to Garrison and thus beyond control by the school board it helped to elect. As long as the possibility existed that Killmer's petition might be denied, this anomaly could not be avoided.

Within about two weeks of the January 25 hearing, two important events occurred. First, the legal advisor for the State Board of Education wrote ESR Board Superintendent Middle to clarify the state's position on the accounting issue: the state had not altered its earlier view that the School Code meant what it said, that "there shall be no accounting made after a mere change in boundaries when no new district is created." Though KCC might argue strongly to the contrary, their annexation to Garrison, according to the law, is "a mere change in boundaries." With regret, the advisor concluded, "this statutory provision contains no exceptions." While this did not preclude appeals to a higher court, it certainly raised doubts about the probability of a prodetachment ruling. Second, the KCC held an open meeting at which it was decided that even though Killmer was trying to detach, they were not yet out of Unit 110, and thus they would have to prepare for the school board election just three months away.

Before and After the School Board Elections: Politics

It is a rare year when a Unit 110 school board election elicits yawns and disinterest; 1977 was not to be such a year. Because two so-called East Side seats (those of Homer Gargan and Herbert Arlberg) were open in the April 1977 election, the KCC decided that two pro–community-school candidates from the East Side must be found. Also in response to the upcoming election a Tipton Concerned Citizens (TCC) group was established, a far cry from the striving, energetic KCC, but still a group that might rally support for opening Tipton's closed school.

As of early March, two East Side, pro–community-school candidates had been located, Sue Hill and Alex Benton, both of Tipton, but the KCC was uneasy about Benton because he had wavered on the issue of opening Killmer's school; a third person, John Trammel of Oldham, they considered a consolidator and thus absolutely unsupportable. The KCC eventually found pro–community-school candidate Marty Harris, a resident of Arlberg's thinly populated Crawford Township. They worried about rejecting Tipton's Benton because he had the

Tipton Concerned Citizens support in the forthcoming election, and they hoped to nurture a possible East-West alliance.

The school board election was scheduled for April 9. All four candidates, Hill, Benton, Trammel, and Harris, attended a final open meeting in Crandall. One after the other, each strode to the front of the room, described who they were and what they supported, and, most significantly, each endorsed the community-school concept. Their endorsements were not equally enthusiastic, but, contrary to past elections, not one candidate so much as hinted at rejection. At this point in time, the candidates reasoned, one could not hope to be an electoral success in Unit 110 without at least voicing some degree of commitment to the concept. Killmer had succeeded beyond its intentions: an open school in each community seemed to have become everyone's issue.

Hill and Harris marched into the election together on a common platform that called for reopening the two closed schools, minimum busing, maintenance of existing buildings, long-range planning, and respect for ''the people's wishes and opinions.'' Both emerged victorious and the Unit 110 school board was ready to be reconstituted. Now, at last, the West Side had a majority; of the old consolidation bunch only Parke and Coler were left.

This moment of clear triumph for Eaton and Killmer raised different questions for each of them. Eatonites wondered: Are the new board members willing to support a decentralized seventh- and eighth-grade organization? Are the children and parents who experienced a centralized junior high school during the 1976–77 school year prepared to return to the smaller, more parochial program of the past? While Killmerites wondered: Are we content to have our school open and remain part of Unit 110? Or should we persist in our effort to secede from Unit 110, regardless of whether our grade school is opened?

To Killmer, defeating Clore in 1976 and replacing Arlberg and Gargan in 1977 with anticonsolidation school board members was a victory marked by a dilemma. The new board majority had to tackle the task of reorganizing the school district.

Killmer's political success assured them that reorganization would be arranged with their interests in mind, but therein lay the dilemma: reorganization surely meant the opening of their school, but, if they got their school opened, would they reduce the possibility of their detachment petition being accepted? That is, would an open school prejudice their case before the ESR Board or any court that considered its petition? Would not such groups reason, "If Killmer's school is open, there can be no warrant for Killmer's detachment?"

Indeed, at their first executive meeting, held ten days after the school board election, the KCC asked themselves these very questions. They sensed that their brothers and sisters in battle had grown weary of the joint struggle to open their school and to secede. Many groused as they opened their purses and wallets to cover additional legal expenses. Some openly doubted the utility of annexing to Garrison if their own school definitely could be reopened. Even their lawyer asked if they really wanted to leave Unit 110 and if there was not now some basis for a compromise. The answer:

KCC member: No, because you can't get a long-term compromise. It [the detachment case] is beyond the point of no return. The board can change its mind any time.

They decided not to oppose any school board effort to open their school, notwithstanding the possible harmful effect on their detachment case.

At its first post-election meeting in mid-April, 1977, the school board elected Joe Kellog president and new board member Sue Hill secretary; it then voted to dismiss the law firm, long in the employ of Unit 110, which had supported Unit 110 at the ESR Board hearing of the Killmer detachment case. The new order had begun.

At its late-April session, the school board passed a motion directing the administration to develop plans for the next school year, including details of budget, class size, and bus routes. Two weeks later, Hart presented the administration's plan; it aroused so much discussion that Walter and Kucera joined Parke and Coler to table further consideration of the plan until the next meeting on May 24. The next meeting was a clutter of involved, tediously debated motions; six of them related directly to district reorganization. Of the six motions (several of them in the form of amendments and amendments to amendments), five were either initiated or seconded by Parke. On three of them, he voted with the minority, which included Sarah Coler each time, once Joe Kellog, and another time Sue Hill. The majority with which he voted included Coler, Walter, and Hill; Coler, Kellog, and Hill; and Coler, Kellog, Hill, and Harris. The old East-West bloc orthodoxy seemed to be eroding. The starting point for this debate was Walter's original motion to have a K–6 in each town and to return Killmer's and Eaton's seventh- and eighth-graders to Eaton. As he had said he would, Joe Kellog abandoned the West Side article of faith—the maintenance of a junior high somewhere on the West Side, at the very least, not in Crandall. He did this in the interest of assuring a K–6 in Killmer.

When your entire house is threatened by a flood, your leaking roof is not a grave concern. For Kellog, the issue of a central junior high school was like a leaking roof, not pleasant, not desirable, but also not as distressing as the water shaking loose your house from its foundation. Kellog perceived a closed grade school as a blow to the foundations of his village. It was a grave and intolerable loss; he felt otherwise about the location of the junior high school. Walter, Kucera, and the KCC did not share Kellog's views. The KCC prepared a handout for distribution at a board meeting which argued for two junior high schools, one at Eaton for the West Side and one at Crandall for the East Side. But Kellog's position got surprising support from students throughout the district. To the distress of their parents, West Side junior high children signed a petition that stated, in effect, "Do not break up the centralized junior high. We like it as it is."

Other voices also were heard in defense of the centralized junior high. Crandall, the sleeping giant, began to stir: at a June 7 board meeting called specially to discuss district reorganization, Ed Schmitt, a Crandall resident, reported the results of a June 1 meeting of Crandall citizens. Over eight hundred persons signed a petition endorsing a K–6 in Killmer and Eaton, a K–2 in Crandall, a 3 in Tipton, a 4–6 in Oldham, and leaving the centralized junior high as is. Schmitt's presentation was followed by a series of speakers from Crandall. They took the petition's provisions as their creed and went on to plead for peace and unity in the district, for putting the interests of the students first, and for parents learning to keep their mouths shut. They claimed that children did not oppose busing; children did not fear Crandall; and children liked the one, large junior high school that had been in operation since September. New sounds, these, and welcome ones to school-district residents satiated with the endless gabble about opening schools and keeping kids out of a central junior high.

In this springtime of change for Unit 110, with its new school board, the promise of reopened community schools, and signs of awakening in the long somnolent East Side, financial problems, the bane of successive superintendents, took a back seat to reorganization. Warren Hart, grown weary with interminable conflict, would not see the resolution of any of Unit 110's problems. Before June 1977 had passed, Warren Hart resigned to assume the superintendency at another Illinois school district where, he said, both the opportunity and the money were better. And where, though he did not say so, the daily torment would be significantly less. Hart's contract had not expired and he was not compelled to leave at this time, but neither he nor anyone else believed that he could operate effectively in Unit 110. On August 7, 1977, at the age of forty-eight, Warren Hart died of a heart attack. He had waited too long to leave Unit 110.

On June 23, 1977, the board, on its third try, passed a motion initiated by Hill and seconded by Parke. It established K–6s in Killmer, Eaton, and Oldham; a K–3 in Tipton; a K–4 in Crandall, and a centralized junior high school. Only Eaton board members Walter and Kucera opposed the motion, diehard K–8ers to the end. Killmer Grade School, closed during the 1976–77 school year, would now definitely be opened in August 1977. The density of events and the intensity of involvement had made the period since February 1976, when the KCC was established, seem like an eternity.

On June 30, 1977, the Educational Service Region Board reported its decision on Killmer's detachment petition. It stated, in the case of Ray Reinhart, the KCC, et al., plaintiffs, vs. The Regional Board of School Trustees of Page County, Illinois, et al., defendants, that granting the detachment petition would not be in the "best interests and educational welfare" of Killmer's students, Garrison school district, or Unit 110.

In the fall of 1977 Killmer's children went to their own community school and to the centralized junior high school and senior high school in Crandall. Killmer township had again failed to secede and annex to Garrison. One more time secession became the dream deferred. Moreover, the dream remained deferred as the KCC's detachment bid failed at every level to which it was appealed, including the state's supreme court.

The defeat of the secession attempt and the reopening of Killmer Grade School mark the end of this chronicle of events in Unit 110, so far as simple narrative is concerned. So far as interpreting the significance of the events or understanding their causes is concerned, however, we have hardly begun.

Perturbations

After one of the late spring board meetings a member of the short-lived Tipton Concerned Citizens said, "When you get your hair done at the hairdresser's, you never talk about school or your hair'll be a mess." The school problems of Unit 110 evoked strong feelings. Indeed, the detachment case preoccupied those who were involved in it, such as the five men I interviewed shortly after the ESR Board rejected Killmer's petition. They are Ned Ruback, member of the KCC executive committee; Tommy Wagemacher, Oldham resident; Tom Middle, superintendent of the ESR Board; and Harve Lander and Ralph Dennison, trustees of the ESR Board. Of course, not everyone in Killmer or even all members of the KCC would interpret and account for issues in the way Ruback does. We must always be cautious in extending the particular feelings and thoughts of one person to other members of a group to which that person belongs. Wagemacher, a prominent man in Oldham, probably comes close to representing the majority point of view in his area, if we judge by voting patterns there and the expressed opinions of other residents. In the case of the three men on the ESR Board, the need for caution is apparent as we hear them give somewhat different accounts of the same event—the rejection of Killmer's petition.

Ned Ruback, Member of KCC Executive Committee

Ned Ruback is not a Killmer native. His interest in the viability of Killmer is eclipsed by his concern for the safety of his daughter. Accordingly, he does not so much ignore the case a Glenn Davids would make for the community school's role in the integration of Killmer as he stresses the community school's contribution to influencing and controlling student behavior. He takes comfort in the belief that in a small town everyone knows everyone else; this means knowing what one's children are doing and with whom they are doing it. Other Killmer stalwarts share his feelings, but may emphasize a different concern to explain why they protest the closing of their school. At the time of my interview with Ruback, his daughter was being bused to Eaton. Though he likes Eaton's school and admires its community, he passionately objects to the loss of control brought about by the busing of his child to Eaton, and he even more fervently objects to measures that promote the cause of centralizing in Crandall any level of schooling earlier than the ninth grade. To Ruback's way of thinking, if it is sad for his child to be bused to Eaton, it would be tragic were she to be bused to Crandall. It is this deep feeling that undergirds his commitment to the purposes of the KCC; it is his commitment, joined with those of similarly impassioned though otherwise motivated persons, that enabled the KCC to persist in its drive to secede.

When Ruback (speaking in March 1977) theorizes about what has been happening in Unit 110, he sounds angry and disgusted:

"The whole thing is going toward a K–12 campus; it started from the day the unit was formed. That idea was in the back of somebody's mind. Gaumnitz and some of them, they had plans way back that Killmer should be phased out. I've always said, 'It's like a train on a track. It's got a destination. The train just doesn't come out and say we're heading for K–12, but the train doesn't get derailed. It may get sidepassed a little bit now and then, but it never gets derailed.' Clore finally came out with it; he finally broke it open [when, as a board member, he advocated a one-campus, K–12 education system]. The K–8ers knew what was going on and we had to educate the people.

"Denton Steed's wife, Alice, we wanted her for our daughter Linda. We ended up getting a first-year teacher for Linda in kindergarten; turned around the next year she got a first-year teacher in the first grade. She got to the second grade and the second-grade teacher said my daughter's class was the biggest class of dummies she'd ever seen. She couldn't believe it. Our kids over there in Eaton now, teachers say if the kids hand in their papers with no names on 'em at all, they can pick the Killmer kids out from Eaton, right and left. A lot of people didn't know we was getting shortchanged; we didn't realize it was as bad as it was. The whole deal was just to let it [the Killmer school] run down. What was happening here was our principal wasn't keeping up on stuff like this. Steeds knew this, see. So we had to get all these people here in Killmer educated. We've got 'em now, we've got 'em educated. They're more educated than any community in Unit 110.

"We feel there's a power somewhere. Hart's background shows he was hired to come here to build a K–12 campus; and that's what Talman was hired for. You elected the board members, but actually the board didn't run it, superintendent didn't run it, somebody else was running it. Hart admitted, after about a year or so, that this unit is not designed for a K–12 campus. We feel this way. If Crandall gets a K–12 campus, who's going to benefit when the K–12 campus is built near or in Crandall? All right, that's the only way we can figure it. Somebody, something, or some group, we feel, gets to so many board members. Denton Steed was fully convinced there was a guy in Crandall that carried the ball all the time and kept up everything. People thought it was Thomas Stoughton. He died, but it didn't stop. We feel it's in the Crandall bank. Just don't know how far to go with this thing; you could get really nasty. The bank holds the loan on people. The next time something goes a little fishy on the board, why you're reminded that you've got that loan, see. We can't prove it.

"Several people didn't want in in this district to start with. You're saddled with four years of high school which is twelve miles away. This is a lot of driving. Towards the last when your child gets a car it helps out, but it's an awful big worry. We're finding out now that bigger isn't the best. We've got dope and sex and everything. This community school, it's the only thing that's a hub or a center, a common thing for everybody in the community. Church isn't 'cause we go to different churches. You'll eventually meet in the school, you'll finally end up at school, 'cause that's the hub.

"The high school is not bad, but it's bad enough. From what I hear, it's got quite a bit of dope in it. More than we need in Unit 110. I hear the kids won't go to the restroom; they hold it until PE. If you want to be a drug addict, you go in the restroom. I'm not saying that we can't get dope in our grade school; we can still get it here. But we've got a better chance of getting a hold on it than I do when my kids go to Eaton or Crandall.

"What I'm getting at is, say, the first graders are here [in Killmer] and the sixth-graders or seventh-graders are also here. All right, the older kid is outside behind the school smoking. First grader sees him, what's he do? He goes home and tells his mom. The moms might even be sisters and you know it's going to get back. First-grader will say, 'I saw Johnny; he was behind the school smoking.' See what's going to happen? Mother calls mother on telephone and says, 'Hey, my boy came home and says your boy was smoking behind the school.' Bango, it's right at home, you know. Control. You don't get that when they get over there [in Eaton or Crandall].

"Another thing that hurts us in Killmer is the radio announcers and everybody uptown [in Pageville] they call it Harmony High School of Crandall, but it is not actually in Crandall, just near it. That is a false statement 'cause we have Killmer boys playing on ball teams. It hurts. I don't know how they feel on the other side [Tipton and Oldham], but in Killmer and Eaton you're instantly mad. There's five towns involved in this deal and one town takes 'er all just 'cause the stinkin' high school's over there. And our kids get no recognition at all. Now that they wiped out our grade school, our kids are nothing. Like this year [1976–77], they don't call it the Killmer-Eaton Grade School; it's Eaton Grade school and Killmer's out. It really tears you up. It's just stuff like this, it really is.

"One thing we can say is we haven't resorted to violence. Now I have heard that board members have received a lot of phone calls. Thought about doing it myself, but I never did. I guess I was trying to be too much of a Christian. I think about it and that's a sin. If you think, you're still just as guilty as doing it. You can only back a person so far. It's like a rat—if you get him in a corner, he's going to fight you, go right for your face. We decided when we formed the group—we were thinking about one guy here in particular that might get off his rocker, get violent, gun happy—we decided we'd better quit talking about barn burning and stuff like that. We might steer somebody wrong sometime. So we only talk about it in very close circles. You don't know, what does it take to get to a guy? What does it really take? You talk and you talk, you plead and you threaten, and you sign petitions and you hand in signatures."

Ruback never misses a KCC meeting and willingly accepts any assignment; these past several years have been a time of anguish for him and his family. But they have not been pleasant for Tommy Wagemacher, Oldham farmer and native, graduate of Unit 110 schools, and father of three girls now attending Unit 110 schools. Like Ruback, Wagemacher has very strong feelings. He is speaking in February 1977.

Tommy Wagemacher, Oldham Resident
"I think that probably things in Unit 110 got out of control at the point when citizens in Killmer first put up the sign with Clore's and Fred Parke's names on Main Street, like these guys all should be hung in effigy. It was up there for about eight months. And this was a ten-by-twelve-foot billboard with mockery signs on it. As far as I was concerned, the ESR Board should have taken legal action against those people. You don't put somebody's name up like that.

"Killmer is a very emotional community. Maybe that's all you can say about 'em—a city made up of feelings. But what right do a few feelings have to affect the education in maybe three other communities? From what I've learned about Reinhart, he's got to be the antagonistic-type person that's trying to salvage his own business. Maybe you could say it's selfish interests, because I think I could present facts to you to prove that one man is financing this situation [Killmer's secession]. Yes, two or three large checks that financed this have been paid out by Ray Reinhart. So it looks to me like we've got the Reeders doing the legwork and the Reinharts doing the paying.

"See, there used to be a East Harmony and a West Harmony Junior High; that used to be a rivals thing. And it was all put together wrong because it should have just been Unit 110. At the school board meetings I go to, there's always a group from every town protecting its own individual rights. Well, Killmer, if you go back and look at the records, no matter what proposal was brought up they'd be the opposite of the rest of 'em.

"This is so complicated. Those people don't dream what's happening. The only thing is those are a bunch of damn poor people on that side, and there's a bunch of people on this side that's money. We could collect $50,000 if we had to fight this thing. It's the haves and the have nots, and yet the have nots have been dominating the feelings of the unit. Killmer's feelings have been dominating the whole unit. My dad once said, 'God help us if Killmer ever gets in a district with people from over here.' That's when I was a kid."

Killmer's behavior antagonizes Wagemacher. He feels its people are cry babies and troublemakers who keep Unit 110 stirred up, and that they are led by a man with only his own business interests at heart, rather than the interests of the school district. Since Wagemacher insists on the integrity of Unit 110, he refuses to see community interests as legitimate. Wagemacher's hostility to Killmer leaves no scope for understanding Killmer's motives. Since he dismisses Killmer as perverse, he relieves himself of the need to take them seriously. From his perspective, Killmer needs to be dealt with, not understood. Killmer's secession would please him, but Harve Lander's view of Killmer's case discourages this possibility.

Harve Lander, ESR Board Member

Harve Lander, like all the other ESR Board trustees, is a farmer and landowner. As a native of Page County, he feels he knows to whom to turn for information about Killmer's detachment petition. He turns to people he can trust, like Unit 110 board president Fred Parke. Satisfied that he and his board colleagues worked diligently to be informed about the petition, Lander is comfortable with how he decided, and what he decided about, its fate (Lander's words were recorded in February and March of 1977):

"The first thing we asked, I remember this quite well since kids are involved, 'What are the educational facilities of Garrison District? What are Unit 110's?' We talked to both district's boards. It was very informal; we respect people's areas. It's coffee shop talk, a private viewing with the president of the school board or the superintendent. It's more or less how we were raised—when some problem comes up, it's worked out between the community and its head office. I worked with Fred Parke, and he kept me informed. If there was anything he felt the ESR Board should know, he called. We more or less go to reliable, good, tax-paying citizens in the community that we feel we can trust, that can be nonpartisan. It's like going to a doctor you can trust, one that won't tell you a bunch of BS or give you pills you don't need. A Garrison board official was on my place about a half a dozen times asking me how I felt about it [the detachment petition] and telling us his personal opinion. So before our decision was ever written up, we pretty much had the general picture of the whole thing. When we went to dinner before our last meeting the board knew how I felt for the simple reason I had brought facts to them, but they didn't know how I was going to vote. We make statements, we back 'em up with facts, and then we go from there. We work strictly with the intelligence of the board members and, boy, they've got it. They'll let you know if they don't like something or they'll ask questions that will blow your mind. I didn't know how the vote was going to be until we were in that boardroom. In fact, I was surprised when two of the board members voted the way they did, 'cause I knew that they had been talked to by Killmer. I call it perjured when you get five or six women that call you five or six times a day. Well, they called me twice and wanted to set up a meeting at their convenience to tell their side of the story. The only facts I intend to hear are the ones presented to me in testimony. Those are the only facts I can take and use to decide. I can't listen to anything as far as propaganda.

"Before we meet we unofficially discuss business over a meal which we pay for ourselves. It's always nice to have a briefing session so actually we usually meet at about 5:30 for a 7:30 meeting and discuss a lot of these things preliminary. There's a lot of table pounding and questions asked and a lot of times we have to make phone calls before we ever get to the meeting at 7:30. You just can't sit down and make a decision unless you have all the input.

"Deep down I would have liked to see Killmer leave. I think that most of the board members would have liked to see Killmer leave because of all the hassle that's been going on in the unit. One of the board members, the first statement he says, 'No matter what we do, they'll go fight. They're going to be unhappy at Garrison, they're going to be unhappy at Pageville, they're going to be unhappy anywhere.' Tom Middle actually looked into them setting up their own unit, and it can't be done [because Killmer fails to meet the state's requirements]. Killmer, they're unwanted.

"I'm convinced that all members on our board feel Killmer definitely has a problem that's out of control. They're being agitated by a fun-loving attorney. We can't prove it, no one's going to talk, but we have a feeling that this [detachment] has been laying around maybe since the beginning of Unit 110. Maybe this has always been the desire—to fight the rest of the unit to get out, to do something different, to just be damn radicals, as far as I'm concerned.

"If I have to point to something as the basis for my decision to resist detachment, well, the majority of our board felt how can we grant a petition to transfer as many or more students into a district than they [Garrison] now have. I asked the question, 'What are we going to do if we move them over there and it doesn't work? What kind of a mess have we made for the Garrison District?'

"We have an identity problem in this Unit. There's no such thing as Killmer, Eaton, or Crandall school district. It's Unit 110 school district. Whatever the board in Crandall decides, that governs the whole unit, not just one town. I'm not saying a thing about towns. But in my eyes, educationally, they don't exist. When you form a school district, the district is the governing body. The town is not. This is how we're educated as board members. I don't think we're going to lose any sleep over whether a town dies or not. We don't look at town problems; that isn't our responsibility. We look at problems of kids, laws, buildings. That's the priorities. I still have to be objective enough to do what is best for the student in Killmer.

"Killmer said they don't want to die. They're saying if you close our school, we're going to die. We don't deal with that; we don't have to deal with it. Why should I worry about a town? I live in a diminishing country out here. How many farmers have left, have been forced out of the community? Did you see any community die? You know what's killing Killmer? The price of gas. People aren't going to drive twenty-five miles to work when they have to pay so much. Why don't we really find out what's killing the towns? There's nowhere in our books says that we have to protect towns.

"I was in the pizza place one night. There was twenty kids came up to me and said, 'Mr. Lander,' and I recognized over half of them was from Killmer, 'don't do it.' That's all they said to me. 'Don't do it. We think our parents are sick.' Some of the parents causing the biggest stink and their kids don't want to leave Unit 110."

Lander joins Ruback in the notion that there is a conspiracy afoot in Unit 110, but this idea is about all that may link those two men. Of course, their agreement about a conspiracy does not truly link them because they differ completely about its substance: Ruback sees one directed *at* Killmer (by the train of centralization) and Lander sees one directed *by* Killmer (with its secessionist propensity). Both acknowledge they "can't prove it"; neither hesitates to speak of it as fact. Given Lander's views on towns and their survival, we understand his refusal to uphold Killmer's petition to detach, though he believes Killmer to be so disruptive in Unit 110 that he would gladly support their detachment if Garrison, by this act, would not face a terrible financial hardship.

Lander's final point about towns is most interesting. The ESR board, he says, has no obligation to recognize the needs of towns as a factor in their decision making; the units of their concern are students and school districts. To those for whom the welfare of the town is the prime issue, Lander's position is incomprehensible. But he believes he is going by the book in that the board's terms of reference do not encompass community survival.

Ralph Dennison,
ESR Board Member

"A school district needs to be able to plan its finances and faculty. [Dennison is speaking in July 1978, a year and a half after the detachment hearing.] Unexpected losses and gains of students do not make this possible. In fact, this point weighed most heavily on my mind; it comes from my own school board experience. I'd be reluctant to think my school district could've had good education when from year to year I didn't know the number of students I'd have, where they were coming from, and the amount of money the district would have. Stability is worth something. I figure that Unit 110 knows better than we trustees what their financial situation is. It's not our prerogative to analyze their financial decision; our only job is that we hold title to all school property in Page County. So if they decide to sell a school, that's part of our work. If they vote to close a school, that's their decision.

"If all the conditions the Garrison board had stipulated [in regard to Killmer's annexation] were fulfilled, I'd have looked at the educational issue. We did look at the courses that were taught at Garrison and saw that high school seniors at Harmony High School would not be able to complete their studies if they went to Garrison High School. At the elementary level, Garrison is good, but there's just not the space or the staff to provide a good academic program for Killmer's high school kids. In fact, we didn't have to decide if the present education that Garrison High School offered was as good as what Harmony offered. The basic facts for us were the amount of space available and the dollars. These were the issues, and from all the evidence, we saw that Garrison High School was not going to be able to accommodate Killmer's high school students.

"I wasn't afraid that if Killmer was granted detachment other places in Page County would also wish to detach. I had to consider the Killmer case in its own rights. I argued for two hours on this point with a Killmer man who tried to convince me that I was going to vote against Killmer because I feared setting a precedent. This detachment case is actually only the second one I've heard in the eight years I've been on the board."

Ralph Dennison is not hostile to Killmer. Like the other ESR trustees, he rejected Killmer's detachment petition, though not, it would seem, without careful deliberation. In his response to Killmer's petition he underscores one particular point: Garrison's stipulations for accepting Killmer could not be met. Had they been met, he says, then other issues would have become central, particularly those related to whether or not Killmer's children would suffer or benefit educationally from annexation to Garrison. In contrast to Lander and Tom Middle (see below), Dennison emphasizes the importance of stability to a school board's capacity to plan and to conduct its business successfully.

Tom Middle,
Superintendent, ESR

Tom Middle's elective position as ESR superintendent is not usually associated with a major political party and it is not hotly contested. In the days before teacher certification required at least an undergraduate degree, and before state-level involvement in education became so extensive, the superintendency was a much more important position. Nonetheless, his role in life-safety decisions and detachment petitions suggests that the superintendent's office remains one of some consequence. Middle came to the job from public school administration. Following his defeat in a recent election, he returned to his old line of work. Among the factors that led to his defeat were his "unpopular" decisions in Unit 110's controversies. For the most part, unpopular decisions seem to be the only kind that anyone can make in a Unit 110 controversy.

Full of opinions without being opinionated, Tom Middle is articulate and forthright in his review of consolidation and secession in Unit 110, a school district he would have preferred was located in any other region than his own (he is speaking in March 1977):

"The Board's overriding consideration, I think, was the curriculum of the two schools. For a youngster presently in the Unit 110 school program, let's say a sophomore, he's got a particular sequence of courses mapped out for a four-year program. If he goes to Garrison, he's going to have to, not alter but major overhaul, his direction—an overhaul downward, not upward. From that standpoint the board felt it was in the best interest of the kids involved (and that's what we're all about) to reject the petition.

"Another thing is where do the people in Eaton and Killmer go for their goods and services? They go to Pageville. So distance in today's way of life isn't all that important. Busing isn't the crucial issue. Herbst played on that tune at the hearing; he really pinpointed it as one of the major problems. Yet Killmer people don't think a thing about getting in their car and going to the Pageville mall to shop. They go farther to buy a loaf of bread than they are willing to let their kid go to get a good educational program.

"Now don't get me wrong; I think the people in Killmer ought to have their school. I've told them that, I've told Superintendent Hart that, and I've said that to the Unit 110 board. I think they have enough people in that town. I think it's a matter of community pride, and pride is a commodity that we need in today's society. I'm not going to say what grades ought to be there, whether it's K–4 or K–6. I'll let the board decide that without interjecting my opinion. I simply think that there ought to be some kind of school program maintained in every one of those communities.

"Fred Parke is a good farmer but he won't compromise. You cannot be a board member and be unwilling to compromise. I don't know if Fred would call me an enemy or not, but, you know, he did some tremendous game playing on the board. Once I was invited down to a board meeting, and Fred came

in and talked to me the afternoon before I went to that meeting.
I told him what I was going to say. I said, 'Fred, this is my
position [on life safety]; it hasn't changed and it's not going to
change.' It was contradictory to what his opinion was and he
used every ploy in the book to keep me from saying that the
board had to get the life-safety work done or we were going
to take measures with the state and reduce their recognition
or take it away completely. Fred sat here and said, 'Well, I
don't agree with you.' And I said, 'If you can show me where
your buildings can be lived with in a safe manner, fine. But I
have all kinds of documentation from your architect, from the
state architect, that these buildings are unsafe.' He thought it
was ridiculous to spend money on them and that there was no
way they could afford to do it.

"Basically my board has said, not in so many words, that
they will be very, very reluctant to allow detachments and
annexations. Still, the mood of our board was such that they
would have allowed Killmer to go to Garrison had there been
any resolution to the financial side of it. The board said many
times during the course of our study session that if there was
any way Garrison could afford to take them, we'd let them go.
They should have been there in the first place. That was the
original plan [in 1948].

"I've got a few friends in Killmer and a lot of enemies,
too. I never would have closed Killmer school. As a school
administrator, I think that was a poor decision, and we can
second-guess Mr. Hart, God rest his soul, but I said so at the
time. Frankly, Mr. Hart was a very poor administrator. Proper
information, consistent information, honest information given
in a consistent way was something they [the school board] just
didn't have. They didn't really know how much they were in
debt. They never really knew.

"I asked a group of people to meet with me who were on
the board way back when it was originally set up to give me
background and perspective on the mess we're in. We sat here
for about four hours one evening and the thing they pointed
out was the lack of stability in the administration of the district.
After Gaumnitz, they lost stability, they lost educational leadership. That district has been fighting itself. It's one half of it
fighting the other half. There hasn't been anyone able to get
the head on the goat and get it doing what school systems ought

to do. You know, I've often said somewhat facetiously, and I don't mean this to be derogatory to anyone, but Christ and twelve disciples couldn't run Unit 110."

"They didn't really know how much they were in debt," said Middle in regard to the Unit 110 school board decision to close Killmer's school. He firmly believes that given appropriate information (and a more effective superintendent), they would not have voted to consolidate further the schools under their guardianship. "For want of a nail . . ." Perhaps he is right; though he probably overlooks the severity of the mutually antagonistic sentiments which characterize the positions of a Ruback or a Reinhart, on the one hand, and a Wagemacher or a Parke, on the other. Reinhart and Parke elaborate their positions below, but we have heard Ruback and Wagemacher and so can begin to understand the sentiments that led to polarization in Unit 110 and caused the ESR Board trustees to entertain seriously the idea of Killmer's detachment.

Middle makes a provocative observation when he says Killmer people think nothing of hopping into their cars to shop at the mall in Pageville. "They go farther to buy a loaf of bread than they are willing to let their kid go to get a good educational program." Carrie Dewack, as we soon will learn, does not doubt she can provide a sounder education for Eaton's (as well as Killmer's) students, but she joins Ray Reinhart in the belief that considerations other than the quality of the educational program also are at stake. Reinhart and Dewack want both the loaf of bread and the education of their young children to be obtained at home.

7

The Conflict Revisited: Dewack, Reinhart, Parke, and Hart

The four persons presented in this chapter are among the most important in Unit 110. Throughout their interviews, I believe they spoke with candor and a minimum of constraint, free of that urge to put one's best foot forward that would have cast a self-serving aura over anything controversial involving them. Each of the four, I am certain, truly sees things as they present them in these edited accounts. Thus we have the world according to Dewack, Reinhart, Parke, and Hart.

Each of the four typifies a central strand in Unit 110's tangled web, both because they occupy positions which make them highly visible and because they are concerned and articulate. Of the four, two have been allied in their reaction to the contemporary events of Unit 110. They are Carrie Dewack, principal of Eaton Grade School, and Ray Reinhart, chairman of the Killmer Concerned Citizens. Both are natives of their West Side villages, long-time K–8ers, and determined advocates of a community school. The other two are more associated than allied, in that they meet at least twice each month as participants on the school board, Warren Hart in his capacity as superintendent and Fred Parke as board member. Their comments make clear that despite their common support of consolidation, the two men are at odds with each other, their relationship having come apart over various past and present issues. Of the four, perhaps only Reinhart and Hart are, because of their positions, inevitably placed at the forefront of events; were Dewack and Parke quiet, retiring persons they could well have been little heard from. Parke, like Dewack and Reinhart, is a native, but, unlike them, works as a farmer; consequently, living in the countryside, he does not share their nostalgic vision of a village home. Indeed, nostalgia seems not to be part of his emotional lexicon. He responds in terms of the abiding present, asking, so to speak, what is cost effective, how can we improve instruction, and, discreetly, what is best for the farmer. He is not a selfish man, but, no less than Dewack and Reinhart, he has his interests. They happen to place him at odds with the latter two; indeed, as they each define their interests, they appear to be irreconcilably opposed.

Ray Reinhart represents those native Killmerites who see the community school not as a dispensable educational adornment, but as the foundation of the village community. He is mindful of the academic claims consolidators set forth for larger, centralized schools, and he rejects them, believing that educators have long made claims for various innovations which later they repudiate.

Warren Hart is the administrator besieged. If he is not blamed as the cause of the school district's problems, he is accused of bungling, of aggravating the district's ideological divisions. If he had prerogatives to exercise which could have changed Unit 110's state of affairs, the chance to use them seems long past, in that the school board has lost its confidence in him. Thus he exemplifies the administrator at odds with his school board who lacks the personal skills or the external constituency that would provide leverage for controlling or circumventing the board. He is like a live moth nailed to a piece of cardboard, which flutters its wings and shows signs of life, but in reality is powerless to change its damaging circumstances. Realizing that he would always be a pinned moth if he remained in Unit 110, Hart made the only decision he could—to find a job elsewhere.

Fred Parke was instrumental in the resignations of Jason Talman and of Warren Hart. In Talman's case, however, Parke ran for the board with the specific intention of expediting Talman's dismissal. He was already on the board when it hired Hart, but with each vote Parke cast on critical issues, he demonstrated his lack of confidence in the superintendent, and thereby pushed him inevitably toward dismissal or resignation. In his account, Hart painfully details a sample of these issues. Though more forthright than other board members who shared his distress over Hart, Parke was not alone in contributing to the split between Hart and the board. Parke, the unmitigated consolidator, became the main spokesman on the board, once Arnold Clore was defeated, for that view of fiscal responsibility and academic opportunity. While urging the West Side to compromise, and confident that he had demonstrated his own willingness to compromise, he relentlessly rejected most decisions which involved spending money. He is an exemplar of the person of unyielding principle who occupies a position of power.

The loss of Eaton's junior high school provides the occasion for Carrie Dewack to reveal the sharp distinctions native villagers make between villages and larger places (such as Crandall, where her "lost" seventh- and eighth-graders have been required to go). Those in Crandall who will have access to Eaton's tender teenagers are not strangers to Carrie Dewack; she knows who "they" are and she does not like what will happen to her students when "they" rather than "we" are in control. Childless herself, she has no youngsters returning home daily to relate what it is like at Crandall Junior High, and so does not hear that nice things occurred and that her worst fears were not realized. She accuses Kellog of voting his dinner table (Kellog has two children in the junior high school)—of responding to the blandishments of his children rather than to the perception of reality which has guided her and other K–8ers for almost a decade.

Reinhart, as the leader of secession, has publicly stated that because Killmer is so far from the center of the district, it has never felt part of Unit 110. Most Killmerites do not

necessarily share this alienated perspective. Like Hart, Reinhart also is disenchanted with Unit 110; he is tired of fighting
seemingly endless save-our-school battles and therefore seeks
a solution in Killmer's exit from Unit 110. And tired sounds
are clearly audible in Carrie Dewack's words, spoken at the
end of an exceptionally trying year. Only Parke shows no sign
of the worn, weary feeling which characterizes the other three,
though in his own way, he has been no less involved for no
less a period of time.

None of these four is a hero; indeed, Unit 110 has no
districtwide heroes. Rather, it has scapegoats and stereotypes,
caricatures and local favorites, in abundance. But there is no
one whose stature transcends village, township, or side.
Neither is any of these four a knave, notwithstanding that they
and everyone else occupying positions of authority have been
much abused. Depending on one's point of view, each may be
charged with being wrong-headed, incompetent, misguided, or
the wrong person for the times. None of them wanted the
conflict Unit 110 was immersed in; each hoped it could be
resolved on his or her own terms, because each had a stake
in a particular solution. Hart had preferences, but he would
have gladly settled for any sort of peace.

These four actors in Unit 110's drama engage each other
in these interviews, less as an artifact of my questions than as
a result of their intense involvement in antagonistic but nonetheless shared school district and community concerns. Their
unwitting reference to each other substantiates events and
points of view described here and elsewhere in this book.

Carrie Dewack, Principal, Eaton Grade School

When I was having a bad time with a daughter who didn't learn anything, I
decided to take her out of Unit 110's schools. Carrie said, "Don't do it. We
need you to fight for the high school [this was in the early 1950s] or we'll
lose everything. I'll take care of your daughter and you take care of the
high school." And she did it. My daughter grew up to become a teacher like
Carrie Dewack.
—Killmer parent

"See this sack! It's eight grams of marijuana. We don't need bigger schools because then I won't find the rat [who brought the marijuana to the school]. We don't want our kids involved in this kind of thing. There's still some of the country feeling here. People want their kids to behave, mind their manners, get basic skills. We oppose a central junior high because there's more to education than home ec and vocational arts, or a good basketball team with only five kids to participate. I'm against throwing more and more kids together and coming up with crap like that marijuana. I don't want the U.S. to go this way. There's no way to supervise as many students and teachers as they have in the central junior high. Teachers there don't pay attention to what goes on outside their classrooms. Kids here say it doesn't make sense to do anything [bad] outside the classroom because all the teachers get after us together. In a big school you can't get the closeness with kids. How can you measure lives in dollars and cents? If we lose our values, what will carry the country?"

The comments above represented my greeting from and introduction to Carrie Dewack, known throughout Unit 110 simply as "Carrie." Most persons in this rural-oriented school district are called by their first name; there is only one "Carrie" in the school district. Waiting for her in an outer office crammed with cabinets, desks, and secretaries, I browsed through bulletin board announcements and expected her momentarily to summon me. The instant I sat down in her office she reached over to grasp a little pouch from a nearby table. "See this sack!" she said angrily, and continued with a tirade against changes in her school district and in American society which appall her. She wore slacks (always does, as far as I know), and smoked. Once she began to talk, I could barely edge a question into her seamless monologue. For she is a passionate woman and the issues we discussed aroused her passion. I don't think she has a meek word in her entire vocabulary. Not everyone in Unit 110 loves Carrie Dewack (to this she would say, "I don't give a good damn"), but no one can be indifferent to her, and no one ever seriously offered a competing candidate for the school district's "best principal." Neither in the fol-

lowing interview nor in the narrative of this book do we observe
her at work as principal, though we hear much about the quality
of her work. She appears, rather, as the communal enthusiast,
championing village life as only a second- or third-generation
native can. Unlike Ray Reinhart, her old K–8 comrade, who
for the past several years has struggled to keep Killmer's grade
school intact, Carrie, because her grade school was not in
jeopardy, concentrated on the junior high school issue—its centralization and location in Crandall. The loss of her community's seventh- and eighth-graders evoked her deepest concerns
about social life in the larger setting of Crandall, the importance
of home-town socialization, and the general decline of discipline, virtue, and order in this country. With ease she slips
from the small world of Eaton and Unit 110 to the large world
of American society; to her, the same awful things are happening in both settings.

The commentary which follows was recorded in May and
June 1977, when the board had a 5-2 majority favoring community schools but had not yet shaped the exact reorganization
plan which it would support. She has just completed her first
year as principal of a school containing only grades K–6. On
the one hand, she is pleased to be released from some respon-
sibilities which attend the principal of a school containing
seventh- and eighth-graders. On the other, she grieves over the
placement of these children in Crandall, where, she believes,
they will be corrupted. Having struggled so long to keep this
age group at home, she feels betrayed by those Eatonites who
once marched at her side but now have succumbed to the lures
of the centralized school's social opportunities.

"I've never been anywhere else and I don't know anything
else but Eaton. I don't know, I've just always been satisfied
where I was. I don't have any desire to see the great places
in the world. I'm happy with what's around me. Even though
I may not have had the finest in home life, this has always been
home. It's where I wanted to be and where I wanted to stay.
I've lived here all my life, so I'm very conscious of what takes
place in this town. I want it to be a certain way and I'm on the
village board to do what I can to keep it that way—not to stop

its growth, but, by God, to keep it a decent place to live. Probably most of 'em on the board are more or less natives, you might say. My brother and I are on it. My dad was on the board, and my grandfather, too.

"I don't think the emphasis today is placed on education in any way, shape, or form like it used to be. The complete 'do your own thing' attitude of everybody in the world today— it seems like everything that was right when I was a kid is now wrong, and everything that was wrong is now right. I know what would have happened to me if I'd been out drinking beer like kids today. I wouldn't have sat down for a month. And the teenage pregnancies—you didn't do that in my day. You were disgraced. Well, now it's the thing to do. Rugged individualism? There isn't any. Nobody wants to conquer anything anymore.

"In the forties when I was in school you didn't roam like kids do today. It used to be that school was the only real place you had to go. There was no movie, no dance hall, nothin' like that. I mean your school was your activity. A lot of people still depend upon the school for that social activity. When we had the junior high here, as long as you had sports activities, you had your parents attend. And when we had our musical, we got a heck of a good crowd. The older people, too. 'Course, I always sent the senior citizens tickets and they came; they thanked me for sending 'em. They can't get out to go to Page- ville, but they did enjoy coming to the local things. People can live without the junior high, you know what I mean, and they're going to continue to live without it, but there's something that leaves a community when your school leaves. I'm not saying it's going to die, but there's a certain something that goes.

"Killmer and Eaton, the ink was hardly dry [on the 1948 reorganization plan which created Unit 110] and they were trying to pull out of the school district. They've always thought that school consolidation is the brainchild of a bunch of college professors and their cockeyed educational theories. And the other thing that caused this side of the district to always be upset was the fact that they thought Crandall wanted the whole school system over there. Small-town rivalry is what it amounts to.

"Why did the board decide to close down these schools in the first place? A seed planted by Mr. Hart. The board would never have closed 'em if he hadn't more or less shown them the way. He told 'em they were broke, and the only way they could exist was to close these schools. Sure, we've got financial trouble, but, by God, we didn't solve a damn thing closing the schools. All we did was make one town go out and spend thousands of dollars trying to get their school back.

"Do you know whether we saved any money closing those schools? I don't; nobody knows. It's too damn complicated for the ordinary person to say because it isn't spelled out. That board has no idea where we are financially. Fred Parke is going to bankrupt us. It's obvious what he's doing making all those motions to put back music, to put back PE, etc. A year ago he was rejecting everything to save money and now I suppose he thinks if we spend enough money it'll force us to go the way he wants to go and then we'll have to consolidate.

"People feel Crandall is getting everything in the way of economic advantages. It's not true, completely, but people believe it. The West Side never voted for a single referendum at any time [Eaton has not; Killmer has]. They protest all change for fear of losing their school and they never want to pay more taxes. These are farmers. But people in the village don't vote yes when they go behind the curtain to vote, even though they yell yes in the open. We've been committing educational suicide all the time because of negativism in the district.

"You know, a year ago Eaton parents were walking the front of this school building with their picketing and boycott signs not to move the junior high to Crandall. And some of those who were the biggest ones for not moving it are the ones now presenting the petition to leave it in Crandall where it's been all this year. In one year they believe another way. Why? Well, their kids like it. Parents evaluate an educational system on whether or not their kids are happy, not on what they're learning or how they act. They gave up on the busing to Crandall because their kids enjoy it. Hell, it's a kid's world anyway; we're just here on a visit. We don't set the standards. The discipline is a lot more lax in the school over there. One girl who left here and went to the high school was ostracized and picked on by a group of Crandall girls. She finally told 'em she wanted to talk to 'em. They met at the high school and she said, 'Just exactly what don't you like about me?' They said things to her like, 'We don't like the way you comb your hair, we don't like the way you dress, and have you ever been drunk, have you had sex, and have you ever used drugs? If you haven't, we don't like you!' I've had another person tell me that kids refer to under the bleachers at the junior high as 'the snake pit' 'cause that's where all the kids go [to 'neck and worse,' so it is rumored]. Boys and girls set their stake-outs to watch for teachers coming. Over there in the junior high, if you don't drink, smoke, or use drugs they call you 'pussy.' "

To the profound dismay of Carrie and others who had persistently opposed all such centralization plans, one year's experience in Crandall's centralized junior high school undermined Eaton's hard core of K–8 support. Carrie felt betrayed, and too weary to continue what now looked to be a thankless struggle with no chance of success. Though at the time of this interview she spoke of retiring, she continues to be principal of Eaton Grade School.

"If the board is going to open Killmer's school, why does Killmer want to withdraw from Unit 110? I'll tell you why: to save face. And also because they don't trust the board. They might open it next year and close it the year after. 'Course, they really have no assurance that if they got to Garrison, Garrison won't close 'em. I think it's become a matter of principle with 'em. Most of this stuff has become a matter of somebody's principles and not the overall good.

"People do make the case that a K–12 is a very ideal school system, that it would save the most money and allow the richest education. Probably it would. But I don't know that that's right either, because I can see where you can get too many in one place and you lose what to me is just as important—personal attention. I feel that at a smaller school you can sometimes rectify or stop kids from getting in trouble. If there's a problem, I can find any parent I want in Eaton and Killmer because I know their hangouts.

"This Thursday at the next board meeting when they plan to settle this reorganization business, here's what they'll do. They'll keep the central junior high, let the East Side have their same organization next year as this year, and reopen Killmer. This sounds like a temporary solution to leave the

East Side as it is, but everything we've ever done has been temporary. I don't care if they want to organize or how they're going to organize, but for God sakes give us a decent place to work in. I wouldn't even fight them on centralization 'cause I've reached the point where I simply don't give a damn. This will never be a unit because nobody cares what happens to the other guy, which is the way society and the whole darn world is going today. Everything you've ever worked for is gone [her K–8 school], so just take it and go. Set it up any way you please, but for God sakes get something and leave it alone. Quit tearing up the kids every year. We cannot go on with this constant bickering."

Carrie has become quite upset from several hours of reliving the events of the past year. In the end she talks to me as though I am the "they" who have inflicted on her a school jammed with children and who have wrought disorder in her school district. She feels the pain of her lost K–8 school in proportion to her profound, abiding attachment to Eaton. As the unabashed, ultimate village partisan, Carrie is thereby precluded from being a robust contributor to Unit 110's educational union. Indeed, Unit 110 seems not to have a legion of partisans, though it sorely needs one.

Ray Reinhart, Chairman, Killmer
Concerned Citizens

He's a nice man if you don't talk to him about education. He acts like the savior of Killmer.
—Crandall resident

He reminds me of the Daley machine, as much force as that man has.
—Oldham resident

When people accuse Ray Reinhart of favoring a community school to protect his business, he gets upset and readily elaborates on the desirability of a community school—in other than business terms. In defence of Killmer Grade School, he mobilized and kept mobilized his fellow citizens in the face of considerable pressure to disband and accept the status quo.

Not a fire-eating patriot like Carrie Dewack, Reinhart explained his attachment to Killmer by stating simply that he was born in Killmer and, having drunk from the village pump, he will probably die in Killmer. He had, possibly, more at stake than Carrie and thus (aided by a very determined committee) carried Killmer's open school and detachment case beyond the point for which most non-Killmerites thought there was either the will or the need to continue. He is speaking in March and April of 1977.

"Back in the sixties when our oldest daughter was in seventh grade we got a letter one week before school was commenced that she was to attend Crandall Junior High School. All the Killmer seventh- and eighth-graders were going to Crandall because of overcrowded conditions here. It made us mad because Eaton wasn't going to go, just us. We was raised up in arms, the whole of Killmer, so the school board backed down. They picked Killmer because they didn't think we would stand up and be counted. That's my first experience of very active involvement. I've been involved ever since.

"Centralizing the junior high—that's been the issue with Killmer and Eaton for the past ten to fifteen years. We won't forget it. They've just been bugging us that this is the way it has to be and it can't be any other way. We've said, 'No, no, no.' If the board had listened to the people, and the superintendent had listened to the people, then we wouldn't have the problems we're having today. Mr. Talman said we could compete in sports with all the larger schools. I didn't think we need to, but their reasoning is that if we get a central junior high, we can have wrestling meets in the seventh- and eighth-grade, a larger band, a better music program.

"I think Hart came to Unit 110 thinking that he could get things centralized. He still thinks that's the best thing for us, but he agrees it's not for Unit 110. I think Hart could have recommended to the board that we have a different [organizational] setup than what the board approved [when it closed Killmer's and Tipton's schools]. He could have been honest with the board and told them all the facts. Maybe they did know all the facts. One of the things was our financial condition. He should have recommended that they go to the people for an education tax-rate increase instead of a building program. If he did it, he did it behind closed doors in an executive session.

"People say about this consolidation business that what's really at the bottom of it is financial interest—people afraid of losing their business community and not thinking about the education of their children. I'll make a living no matter what. My retail business will go way down [if Killmer Grade School stays closed]. It takes young couples to buy things in the store. If it wasn't for my roofing and siding business, I could not afford to be in the retail business. I still don't depend on Killmer for a living. It's not financial interest on my part. People that are involved in the Killmer Concerned Citizens have nothing financially to gain. We're worried about our community, our community as a whole, not just saving Main Street. If we lose our school, we're not going to get young couples to move here. We'll be a retirement community. When people find out the handicaps of driving back and forth to Crandall or Eaton, they'll just as soon live there. It's a matter of economics to them. The people in our business district are not involved in any of our school activities; they're too busy making a buck. The business interests in Crandall—people here feel like they're part of the push for everything centrally; a lot of people feel that it would be a selling point for real estate in Crandall.

"You could ask some of the board members their reasons for closing our school and you won't get a straight answer. Tom Middle told us there was no excuse for closing Killmer school. He knows that Unit 110 is not that bad off financially. His ESR Board voted against us because they didn't want to open a can of worms. They had their minds made up before we even went in to the hearing. They couldn't say yes because Harrison would want to leave its school district; Danbury might want to get out; and if we got out they would have a precedent for getting out. You won't be able to get the ESR Board to admit that.

"Whenever a school district is having financial problems, what do they all do? They say we've got to cut out sports, cut out band. I don't care which state you go into, they all use the same tactics: they threaten and from that they go on to get support for centralizing. That's the club, right, and that it's best for our children. All you've got to say is, 'It's best for our children.' They haven't proved it to me. I think our children desire not the best, they desire the opportunity for a good education. There's so many things they can learn from the community school. They can be part of the community and still learn. It may cost us a few dollars more, but I think we're willing to pay that.

"When you get out 75 and 80 percent of the registered voters [for a referendum or a school board election], you're doing something that's not done in most places. And when you have to do that year after year to protect your interests, people get kind of disturbed. That building across the street [Killmer Grade School]—it's an old building. They told us it's ready to fall down. It's a firetrap. Well, I don't believe that and I don't think it's because I went to school there. We have an old house and it's not a firetrap; it's not going to fall down. They use tacks like, 'Well, you've got to think of your children.' We do think of our children. 'The kids'—that's the only argument that they use. Well, that and quality education. But what is quality education?"

Fred Parke, School Board Member, Crandall

Parke was extremely smart. One time he said he wanted all schools brought up to the level of Eaton. Equal education? No, all sham to weigh down the budget so it just couldn't be passed. He made it sound good, but I saw through it.
—Former Unit 110 school board member

To say the least, Fred Parke stirs up controversy. At board meetings, when he sits in one of the large, black, thronelike chairs (a Jason Talman legacy) reserved for board members, he looks imposing. He is much larger than most men and he seems always to look stern and unsmiling. It is hard to associate the relaxed, congenial Parke at home with the formidable Parke at board meetings. As we talk, he tends patiently and tenderly to his young son, ill at the time, pausing in his comments to respond to the boy's need for attention. Fred Parke is a successful grain farmer; his fields abut his newly built house. Around him are his neighbors' fields, the distant dots of their houses, and lots of space.

Since Parke has been at the center of Unit 110's major, disputed school board decisions, he often is the focus of attack. For the most part, the masses of district residents who packed board meetings month after month, were hostile to him. Yet, as he recalls the many years of his board tenure, he never responds in terms of this hostility; undefensively, quietly, he describes and explains what he remembers doing and why he did it. His comments were recorded in June 1977 and July 1978. Parke begins with the K–8 group because, paradoxically, they were instrumental in electing him to the board when Talman was superintendent and had aroused the ire of West Side parents. The K–8ers were pleased to have Parke join their anti-Talman cause; they soon regretted his presence on the board. In subsequent elections Parke did not need the West Side votes to gain reelection to the board, nor did he get them.

"The K–8 committee, they met off and on for several years, even prior to my becoming a board member. It's a group that meets just when things aren't going their way in the school system. They're not afraid to talk to board members and tell them what they think. The petitions for the board election were due on a Friday [the first time he stood for election] and I think it was on the Thursday before they were due that I decided to run. The first group of people that invited me to state my views was the K–8 committee from Eaton. I told them I was a junior high, not a K–8 person. But so many other things they were concerned about at that time also were my concerns, so they supported me for the board. The last time around [the last time Parke ran for the school board], the K–8ers were tooth and toenail against me. The difference was the junior high situation. I had told 'em my position the very first time, but it had never really become an issue until later. If it hadn't been for their support, I'd have never been elected the first time.

"At that time, primarily Mr. Talman's leadership bothered us. I think the K–8ers really felt that he wasn't aware of the needs of the communities, at least their community. Mr. Talman had the board ill-prepared for meetings; financially, I don't think that he even realized what was going on. Anyway, finally we were able to get rid of him. The night it came down to the vote on Talman's contract, it was very difficult for me to vote against him. Just something inside of me didn't want to have to take a man's living away from him. Maybe he could have survived as a superintendent in Unit 110 had he not had his little social club that met prior to the board meetings. I mean he was almost running a gestapo.

"Warren Hart's number one priority when he was hired was to update the board's policies. He did an excellent job at it. If he did have certain ideas, he was not strong enough to get the board to buy them. He was not hired with any understanding that he was supposed to consolidate. The initiative to consolidate did not come from Hart. Consolidation—that's just how we think; it's the answer to our financial problem. Warren Hart would say many times that consolidation in general terms is the answer, but not in Unit 110 because the people won't accept it. I was undoubtedly angry with him [in spring 1977] for saying this, but that's not the reason I was against rehiring him. For several years·as president of the board I'd be called in for a conference. He'd find out what position I was going to take on an item and, if that was contrary to his, he'd figure out his flight plan. He'd learn my position and that gave him time to counteract it, to think of something else. That's why I was against him. He tried to satisfy everybody. Warren did an awful lot of telling people what they wanted to hear.

"The people from Killmer just kind of like the kids at home. Apparently, it's a community. Their school is the one thing that the whole community can be behind, where they can come together as a community. They don't want to give that up. That's just what I pick up from what the people say; I don't see that as much as I hear it. They've always enjoyed their school, school programs, fund-raising projects. My personal opinion of those events is it's always really tough to even go to one of 'em. If they want ten dollars out of me, I'd just as soon given them ten dollars as to go down there and eat a bowl of chili.

"Killmer and Eaton—I can't say that they're any different from the other towns other than the fact that they get concerned about issues, and they work toward what they want. It's historically proven that Crandall doesn't care. Primarily the communities are all the same inasmuch as the people live in Crandall or any of these other bedroom communities and commute to Pageville to work. Crandall people, they're more will-

ing to let their kids run the streets. I can't agree with that and
I can't disagree with that. Crandall has grown more than the
other communities, has more move-ins, has less natives, so
to speak. Natives are probably different from move-ins in
community pride.

"We're not really part of the community up here [in the
countryside where he lives]. We, ourselves, don't trade in
Crandall. Our groceries are purchased in Pageville and our
church until little over a year ago was in Pageville, so we didn't
have that oneness with the community or the nucleus of friends
to be with at any of the school events. We didn't have boys
in the Little League; we didn't have anything other than the
kids in school to draw us to Crandall. . . .

"There was an alternative to closing those schools in Killmer and Tipton in 1976. Yes, Killmer didn't have to be closed,
necessarily. I think I'm about 99 and 95 hundreds percent the
reason for that. In the early part of the discussion I can remember Kellog saying that we've got to attack the problem
where the problem is. And by that he meant Tipton, which
didn't have enough students to have a school. I believe that
anything that happens on the East Side to change the situation,
the schools, the boundaries, whatever, is done as a temporary
solution, but it becomes permanent. And my position was that
it's no longer up to the East Side of this unit to sacrifice for
the sake of saving money without some type of sacrifice from
the West Side. I was not going to close the doors of Tipton if
they're not going to close Killmer.

"The board went beyond its recommendation [from Hart]
when it closed Killmer as well as Tipton. I thought there would
be a very upset bunch of people in Tipton if only their building
had been closed. To be honest with you, I felt that this was the
lesser of two evils, which it probably didn't turn out that way.
I honestly thought that we would have many upset people and
in a few months it would probably die down, but it continued
to flourish in Killmer. Now, at this point [July 1978], I'm not
sure that that was the right thing to do. Undoubtedly it wasn't
from the reactions we've had. The continuing fight over
detachment—as far as I'm concerned that's a real problem for
both school districts [Unit 110 and Garrison] to be facing. I
still think we've got to consolidate to hold down expenses.

"The reason Killmer's pursuing detachment is they realize how easy the board can change. They've got control of the board now [following the April 1977 election], but they realize that that can change, and once again Killmer might be closed. They'd just kind of like to see the thing settled once and for all. In my own mind, I don't feel the community over there feels that strong about leaving. They got petitions signed, but that doesn't mean much to me. I really and truly feel that there's probably closer to only 25 to 30 percent that honestly wanted to sign it. I've heard several people say they felt they were forced to sign because, you know, their neighbor brings the petition by and says, 'We really want you to sign this thing. We need your signature.' I understand the KCC people come around 10:30, 11:00, 11:30 at night waking people up to get them to sign. I really don't think that many people in their own hearts and minds feel that that is the right thing to do. I said something to a woman about her brother-in-law signing. She said, 'Oh, he's got to live over there.'

"At the Tipton board meeting [June 1977], we approved a K–6 in every town. I fought that; I was able to stall the decision for about two hours that night. And curriculum was part of the reason. I argued that, 'Are you going to tell me a school in Eaton and Killmer is all you're concerned about, and that you can't be concerned about the curriculum?' Kellog did have the votes to reopen the schools, but he could see that there was going to be an A-1 fight against him increasing the education fund if he didn't keep the centralized junior high.

"I really and truly believe that if my position had won on the financial situation, we'd be a whole lot better off today. The financial problems were starting when I first became a board member. That's what motivated me to get on the board in the first place. It just didn't appear that the true feelings of the community were being considered. I just felt that some honesty and some real feelings from citizens would be helpful. Farmers, for example, are much more concerned [than non-farmers] about how their taxes are spent. This ground that we farm, we've got to pay the taxes on that before we can make dime one. If they would tax my income [rather than the amount of land he owns] that would put it in a different perspective. If the whole tax structure was changed . . .

"I'm not just 100 percent sure what it means when some-body says that the school is the center of the town—maybe because I live in the country, not in a city or in town. There's an awful lot of mothers that load up the kids and take 'em to school in the car. I suppose that's a form of identity, you know, taking these kids some place. They see a lot of other mothers there (and fathers), and have PTAs and all, where they can all get together. Getting the kids to the school and what their kids bring home from school means an awful lot to the parents. For that reason I suppose that's the center of the community then.

"It may be funny, and sad, too, when you think about my position. Several families of friends from Eaton don't visit us anymore because of my position as a board member and their position as what they want for their schools. I can't afford to be a board member any longer 'cause I won't have any friends left in Crandall either. I accept people's opinions for what they are; apparently, people can't respect mine. Most of the time those people on the West Side thought that there were several people conniving to tell me what to do, that I was just a mouth for somebody else. And they even considered Floyd Sycamore, the president of the bank there in Crandall, as telling me what to do. Sycamore never told me what to do. My wife never told me what to do. I mean we'd discuss things a lot of times, but if I didn't agree with her, she didn't get to first base with me. I take the point of view that I represent the entire district. The whole district voted for me. I really feel like my decisions have been based upon the well-being of the total unit. You know, I've always been a loner in this thing all along."

> *Peshkin:* Anything else you think I ought to know?
> *Parke:* No, except when you mention my name say that I am not part of a conspiracy.

Here in these paragraphs is the essential Parke: he reduces the school events that evoke rapture in Dewack and Reinhart to an eminently dismissable bowl of chili parading as a feeble excuse to raise money; he minimizes the size of Killmer's support for secession; and he describes his own geographic and psychological distance from any community. Parke does not speak the same language as Reinhart and Dewack. Unfortunately, no one inside or outside the school district was available to serve as interpreter for Unit 110's fractious groups.

Parke acknowledges that it was not principle but, in retrospect, misplaced sensitivity that led him to urge the closing of Killmer's school. Parke's "lesser of two evils" decision proved to be a sad, costly mistake. It is difficult to understand how he could believe that the historically passive Tipton would react as Killmer and Eaton do when threatened, or that Killmer and Eaton would let the matter "die down." The impression Parke gives here of having second thoughts come from comments he is making more than two years after he and the board majority voted to close the two schools. At no time, as the board debated the issue, did he ever hint that he might act otherwise, unlike Arlberg and Coler, who at times would sound equivocal, even though they seldom changed their vote.

Once Arnold Clore of Oldham left the school board, Parke became the spokesman for the consolidators. He never wavered, though he was tested repeatedly by motions and pressure from the West Side, the KCC, Superintendent Tom Middle, and the state (over life-safety work). How ironic to consider that the enormous efforts of individuals and groups in Unit 110 during the school years 1976–78 could have been avoided had Fred Parke not been motivated by a unique concept of parity: to solve a financial problem close Tipton, to avoid a political problem close Killmer. Parke's decision is perhaps best understood against the background of disparity between East and West mentioned previously: whereas East Side primary school children had been bused since the early 1960s, West Side children remained comfortably ensconced in their precious community schools. Moreover, Eaton had benefited significantly from the leadership of its industrious, assertive principal. Parke, fully aware of Eaton Grade School's advantages, once made a motion that all district grade schools should be brought up to its standard. In short, Parke was vexed by the West Side's material benefits and tried to insure that school board decisions would not worsen the inequities that he believed already existed between the two sides.

The irony is further sharpened by facts that Parke himself presents. "Killmer, . . ." says Parke, "apparently it's a community." Unlike Reinhart, Parke did not grow up knowing, almost instinctively, the special place a school has for people in its host community. Yet he has so often heard the community-school line that he is prepared to believe that there is "something there," only he is not certain what it is, and whatever it is, he does not support it. "As for Crandall," observes Parke, "it's historically proven that Crandall doesn't care." Thus we know that Parke is fully conscious of differences between the two parts of the school district, but he does not support policies that take account of these differences.

The commitment of Clore, Arlberg, and Coler to taxpayers (farmers) emerges fairly clearly from their accounts. In Parke, no less successful a farmer, this commitment does not emerge with equal clarity or force. We see, rather, a mixture of concerns and interests. Do they overlie Parke's fundamental sensitivity to the farmer's condition? It is hard to say from the picture of himself that Parke presents. Even he may not know, given that we so often do not expose to ourselves, let alone to others, the possibly unattractive truths that impel our behavior. At this point, and notwithstanding Parke's awareness of the contribution of his leadership to conflict in Unit 110, he appears to have no misgivings about anything he did. In fact, the leaders of both sides appear to have no misgivings about anything any of them did.

Warren Hart, Superintendent, Unit 110 School District

I forgot who told me, but somebody said closing Killmer was a personal vendetta of Hart's. Somehow, Killmer had embarrassed him. Knowing Warren as I do, I can say, yes, it is possible he had that revenge in his heart.
—Former Unit 110 school board member

"The famous K–8 group called me over for a meeting—it must have been in November of my first year [1972]—and they questioned me at length about my philosophy. I can remember saying to them, 'Look, we don't agree philosophically, but we can still be friends.' And they said, 'Yeah.' They probably understood Hart's thinking and the word filtered back that he believed in centralization. I did not feel that I'd been hired with an invitation to explore consolidation. The board that hired me asked me if I believed in consolidation and my answer, of course, was, 'Yes, I do.' They asked me to take a look at the high school and see if it was overstaffed. I said, 'Yes, I think you're overstaffed.' In that first contact with the K–8 group we visited about the fact that they wanted to keep a K–8 open in every town. They were very open. I said, 'People, you can't justify that.' And I tried to show that the more grade levels we could get together [in one building], the better job we could do. They wouldn't buy it; never have, never will."

"Go back to the beginning," I invited Warren Hart. "What do you recall about getting started in Unit 110?" How appropriate that he begins with reference to the K–8 group and their philosophy. True to form, soon after Hart's arrival, they invited him to a meeting to set forth their beliefs; no less true to form, Hart set forth his beliefs—of course he supported consolidation, and hoped "we can still be friends." His wish to be friends with everyone may well have been his undoing; he undercut his own credibility by appearing indecisive, unwilling to back up unequivocally the positions he took. By both believing in consolidation and rejecting it as unsuitable for Unit 110, he thereby landed himself in the middle, where he did not manage to "still be friends." On the contrary, he managed to antagonize people on both sides of the fence he was straddling.

In the course of many long meetings with him (chiefly in November 1976 and February 1977), he described incident after incident with the board which vitiated his authority and cast the board in an increasingly larger role in Unit 110's administrative process. As discrete events, they were not of major consequence; their accumulated impact, however, denied Hart the capacity to exert a desperately needed leadership role in his cloven school district.

"The first year I was here the board was split 4-3 against retaining Goshen, the high school principal. Clore, Arlberg,

Ellis, and Gordon—these four board members, all Talman supporters, were at odds with him about issues left over from
Jason Talman's days. When I got here the two sides visited my
office quite frequently trying to sway me to their way of thinking. When I recommended Goshen be reappointed as a junior
high [rather than high school] principal, he called the state
principal's association in for an investigation, which he had a
right to do. Their recommendation to Mr. Goshen after their
visitation was, 'Get out.' That made the pro-Talman element
on the board happy. The three that supported Goshen [includ-
ing Fred Parke], they accepted it because the investigation had
been held.

"Then Mr. Parke kept saying to me, and I wasn't smart
enough to pick it up, 'What are you going to come up with
next?' He was the president and I'd meet with him and go over
the agenda before the meeting to give my thinking and get his
thinking. He kept saying to me, 'What are you going to come
up with next?' Well, I should have picked up that he really
didn't trust me.

"At the end of my second year, when the board went into
executive session [to discuss a high school teacher who
squirted some kids with a fire extinguisher], we never did get
to the problem because Mr. Parke began to criticize me. I didn't
understand it because I thought Mr. Parke and I had a tremendous relationship. The next day I called Fred—I'll say this
about him, he's a very honest individual—and I said, 'Fred,
what turned you against me?' He says, 'When I come in here,
you tell me one thing; when somebody else comes in, you tell
'em another thing.' I says, 'How do you know?' 'Well, that's
what they're telling me.' I says, 'Fred, are they telling you
what I said or what they wanted me to say?' I told him, 'I'll
accept your vote, but you're going to accept me as superintendent.' He says, 'That's right.' So we left it right there.

"Eventually we evolved to a 7-0 board and we worked real
congenially until money problems began. I can see when the
board started taking over the administration. I made a proposal
to close the old Tipton building. The board approved that one
meeting and two meetings later rescinded it because of pressure
from the local people. I took the blow. I said, 'Well, they're
not ready for it; let's go on.'

"Then we brought in a basketball coach. OK, it came time to reemploy staff and the board voted 6-1 to fire him. This was against the principal's and my recommendation. I asked why. Mr. Parke said you can't evaluate him because he's a personal friend of yours. Well, I resented that very much, and Mr. Parke and I had words right then. 'Cause if I can't have a personal friend and still evaluate him as a teacher, I'm pretty damn poor.

"Well, this was in January, and in April Mr. Parke chose not to be reelected president of the board. At the meeting to choose a new president, we went into executive session to talk to our attorney. I don't even remember the problem. Mr. Parke asked him, 'How do we fire a superintendent?' My response, and I remember that very directly, 'With 'a hundred thousand dollars, Mr. Parke. That's how you fire me.' And right then the split was there and it's still there. When Mr. Parke and I split, that split me and the board. That's when Arlberg and Clore and Parke started getting close together. When I came here, they wouldn't even speak to each other.

"This same meeting I just mentioned, where we were voting to reemploy staff, was being held in Eaton. Prior to the public part of the meeting, the board fired Carrie Dewack on a 4-3 vote. It just happened; it wasn't planned that way. When it came time to make the motion in public to reemploy her, Harry Walter made the motion and the Killmer member seconded it; each of them always does this. It came to vote and I knew it was 4-3 against her. We had five hundred people sitting in those bleachers (I'm exaggerating a little). When the board started to vote in public, I'm frankly in my chair about like this. [To demonstrate, he sits on the edge of his chair with one leg forward as though he were preparing to bolt.] If the fourth 'no' vote comes, I'm going to get out of there right away. Homer Gargan changed his vote to reemploy her and saved a riot on our hands. Now not professionally they were letting her go, 'cause she does her job. She helped to get rid of Mr. Talman, and they [the board's pro-Talman supporters] were going to get her.

"Fred Parke is a bright young man; don't really understand him. I don't think there's another board member that could have been president of the board and kept order through this last year [1976–77] of utter chaos like he did. He has no confidence whatsoever in me; he's told me that. I haven't told him

yet that I don't have any confidence in him, either, but I will
the next time we meet. He has not voted to reemploy teachers
or for teacher raises in the four years I've been here. His
comments to the public is we have some weak teachers and
he will never vote to reemploy weak teachers. But when the
teacher's been here twenty years, even if he is considered a
little weak, you're not going to get rid of 'em.

"As for the other board members, Harry Walter wants a
K–8 in every town and he hasn't budged one bit since I came
to Unit 110. Walter leads the people—when they want something done in Eaton, Harry Walter is the one they give it to.
Joe Kellog works in the electrical plant up at Pageville College;
got on the board basically to preserve the Killmer school. You
won't see him vary from that. Joe communicates with his citizens. When he started out on the board, he got extra copies
of the agenda to post in Killmer's post office and school caf-
eteria. He does ask the people what they think; he takes his
role seriously. Kellog and Walter just want a K–8 at any cost;
they try to cut back the high school to the basics. Nobody in
the district will rally to support the high school. Homer Gargan
is secretary of the board; he works for Pageville Roofing as
their supply man. He's for centralization. About the time he
was a student, counties around here were closing rural schools.
He rode a bus. After football practice, he got home the best
way he could. He sees nothing wrong with busing students. I
appreciate Homer very much. He's the type of individual—
used to be, I haven't tried it lately—when I wanted to get
something done, and needed a real strong supporter on the
board, I'd call Homer and say, 'Let me buy you lunch.' So I'd
take him out to lunch and I'd say, 'Now, damn it, this is what
needs to be done, Homer, let's get it done.' OK, no sweat, and
we'd get it done. At that particular time, he and Fred Parke
communicated before every board meeting to decide what to
do. Those two could carry the ball for me. Homer is biding his
time right now because he's fed up with it [the board and what's
happening in the school district]. I don't know where Sarah
Coler stands. She's only been on a little over a year. Herb
Arlberg is centralization all the way. Hasn't changed in the five
years I've been here. Still, he's willing to compromise if what
the people want is a K–6 in every town.

"I favor a central junior high, but the West Side want their kids to stay home as long as possible so they can teach them their values. These kids have got to be prepared for the outside world. How much would local values be lost if we had a K–12 school somewhere out in the country? Not so much, I think. Miss Dewack doesn't want Eaton to change; she wants her values to prevail. When her kids get to the high school she puts in the Eaton Grade School bulletin the kids from Eaton who made the high school honor roll. She calls me up each year to find out what Eaton kids are on the first team. This year there were none and she didn't come to any games.

"The Killmer Concerned Citizens group say that their school is the center of their social activities. I can vouch for this. At the Killmer awards banquet—and I went to it every year until we closed the school—everybody in town came. Everybody. The biggest potluck you can imagine. Ray Reinhart said to me last spring, 'You're going to take this away from us, aren't you?' That's the most important thing they've got and everything is right around that. 'See what you're doing to the community,' Reinhart said in effect to me. They made me feel welcome, but they took the opportunity to say, 'Look what you're doing to us.'

"Teachers are very fearful that after the board election [April 1977] they'll lose the Killmer and Eaton youngsters back to the junior high in Eaton. I've had five or six parents say to me, 'If Killmer's reopened, can we keep our [grade school] children in Eaton?' You see, Killmer kids are way behind. They're not lacking in ability; they've just always been behind. It's a community factor.''

An Eaton Grade School teacher reacted to the same point. He said five of his eleven fourth-graders from Killmer could not sit still, never having learned to do so because of the frequent turnover of teachers and principals in Killmer. This year, he said, "Killmer parents have told me that for the first time their kids have known what they should do." And a Killmer parent and member of the KCC executive committee confirmed this judgment about Killmer's students. Her daughter never before did homework or "buckled down. Under Carrie, the teachers and kids work.''

"These are some background things. The bitterness is there; the distrust is there. We've developed a distrust here, and, frankly, it's just been damn hard to overcome. Every board member's got it; all the principals have got it; the president of the local teacher's association has got it. I told the board recently that right now I'm at the stage where I don't even like myself. I've always prided myself—come to the office early, you know, keep the board informed of everything, work late, put in hours. 'Gentlemen,' I said, 'I've got a good reason for leaving the office early every day on account of my mother-in-law's in the hospital.' When she's gone, the way I feel, I'll find some other excuse. I don't like Warren Hart and what he thinks of himself. For the benefit of everybody, I say that I've got to get out of here.

"On January 27th [1977], I indicated to the board that this was the end. There was stone silence for two minutes. If I can't find a job I want, that means I'll have to stay here, but they know I don't want to. One board member said, 'Warren, it doesn't make any difference who is sitting in your chair. We're split 4-3, and if we're not split 4-3 one way, we're going to be split 4-3 the other way. The new man will have 90 days, 120 days, and then they'll come down on him.' "

Is it not fair to conclude that a group is known by its leaders?—not in full measure, of course, but at least to a significant degree? To be sure, with the exception of Hart, the leaders described in this chapter all had major allies with whom they operated; some of these are characterized in earlier first-person accounts. But if we know nothing more about Unit 110 than what these four did and believed, and, that they are starring actors in Unit 110, we have gone a long way toward comprehending the cycle of events that seems to recur perennially and to transmit shockwaves throughout the northern half of Page County.

Behind their surface differences, such as Carrie's salty, moralistic language, Reinhart's quietly nostalgic reminiscences, and Parke's frank and detailed recollections, lie several critical commonalities. All three are determinedly, perseveringly righteous about their own causes, aware of their opponents' causes, occasionally even acknowledging their propriety, and nonetheless capable of doggedly pursuing their own. It may be their capacity for single-mindedness, in the face of perplexing contradictions, that enables them to maintain their leadership positions. Other persons in the school district, disciples of neither this nor that side, would be confounded by these contradictions, and confused by seeing the supposed virtues of the community school pitted against the supposed calamities of consolidation. Many have resolved their confusion by rejecting both sides, their decision informed by the feeling that as much as both sides insisted the welfare of children was a foremost concern, the children were indeed being neglected. The truth of this charge is less important here than the fact that belief in it led to a constituency for a return to some manner of normalcy.

I am struck by the insight of many in Unit 110, both the bystanders and the key actors, but I am equally struck by the nearly perfect incapacity of anyone to do more than announce their insights. The occasion to incorporate them into policy and practice was overwhelmed by the raging partisanship which characterized all groups but the powerless Citizens Advisory Committee. Thus the district missed the opportunity, for example, to capitalize on Carrie Dewack's solemn observation that "We've been committing educational suicide all the time because of negativism in the district." Each of the four contributed in his or her own way to this saga of principle and partisanship run amok.

Social conflict, of the sort that Parke referred to in his account, may last as long as damaging stories, unconfirmed and usually without any identifiable source, continue to circulate. In the absence of credible leaders and data, such stories proliferate. No one is immune; the more prominent the person, the greater the number of stories they inspire. Although individual relationships here and there were disrupted by the Unit 110 controversy, Killmer village bore the brunt of the district's negative feelings. Even non-Killmerites who endorsed the community-school concept found it hard to sustain that measure of objectivity and dispassion which would permit them to see Killmer as "victim." Of course Killmer saw itself as "victim," but others perceived their continued fight as obstreperous, excessive conduct. Rankled persons commonly blame the victim for the victim's problems. "If they had only approached the board in the right way"—this type of thinking typified those who believed Killmer had gone too far. Killmer was right, so it was said, to want their school reopened, and wrong in the way they went about it. Accordingly, they earned the label "radical"; their behavior had surpassed the limits of acceptability.

Many people believed that if Killmer had behaved more moderately, both the problems and the disunity of Unit 110 could have been redressed. They interpreted Killmer's pursuit of secession as an attempt to blackmail the board. Arlberg's long pause, after he was asked if he wanted Killmer to remain part of Unit 110, reveals the ambivalence so many came to feel about the village that always fought back. A woman from Oldham was not alone in thinking that

> Unit 110 should never have been set up the way it was. Killmer should have gone to Garrison; it should go now. I wish they would. They seem so selfish, so unwilling to think of the unit as a whole. I'm sure they don't think that way, but that's the way it appears.

Sentiment against secession's disruption of ties that were over three decades old was expressed mostly by older residents who remembered their dreams of a new, large union of schools that would fulfill the promise of a modern education unthinkable in the tiny, pre–union school districts. This dream had a limited circulation in 1948; it was almost ancient history thirty years later.

To the regret of everyone associated with Unit 110, conflict never became ancient history. Those of a conspiratorial mind could point to the consistent behavior of unknown evildoers as an explanation for this conflict. Finding no basis for a conspiratorial outlook, I must look elsewhere to account for what is going on in this distressed school district.

8

Unit 110's Imperfect Union
The Conflict Explained

Even in a milieu marked by rapid social change, men seize opportunities for forestalling and minimizing personal change; they appear to establish, with at least partial success, islands of stability.
—Anselm Strauss, *Mirrors and Masks* (1969)

Senator Black was right in his claim that the "local man" was passing. . . . The American population adopted mobility as normal.
—Daniel J. Boorstin, *The Americans* (1974)

Unit 110's oldtimers never weary of restating their one-line legends: "We fought for years to establish an acceptable high school site, but in the end no one was pleased." "We [the village of Killmer] never really wanted to join them [the rest of the school district] in the first place; you know, the vote to join passed only by a margin of one." "It all goes back to the very formation of Unit 110." The "it all" that goes back is the seemingly endless discord of Unit 110; the legends refer to the origin of this discord, in which Killmer has been central as it endeavors to maintain its island of communal stability.

Both while I was actively involved in the events of the school district's current discontent (1976–79) and as I was preparing this narrative I would think, "Don't get carried away in the presentation of this account, because no one will believe what you say. The long chain of mishaps and misadventures which were the norm in Unit 110 will sound like overwritten fiction to an outsider." Being "carried away" seems to be a common component of the actions and reactions generated by the closing of a school. Surely, I would sometimes think, this whole story is a tempest in a teapot. Can't Killmer's protest be explained quite adequately by the law of physics which indicates that once a body is set in motion . . . ? This law would suggest that once the Killmer Concerned Citizens initiated a movement to detach from Unit 110 and join the neighboring school district of Garrison, they set in motion activities that would continue until stopped by some external force or by the exhaustion of their own motive force. The theory can be stated another way: once the KCC made public its commitment to detach, pride precluded their relenting. I do believe that people get trapped in positions from which they cannot extricate themselves and that this may account partially for the behavior of some persons associated with the KCC.

There are other explanations of Killmer's protest. Some people relish a good fight, and the school-closing episode, if nothing else, was certainly a good fight. And it is entirely possible that the persistent, systematic pursuit of secession resulted from the fortuitous assemblage on the KCC executive committee of people with great energy and great organizational skills. Undoubtedly, a KCC without Ray Reinhart would have failed.

Finally, some may put stock in one school-district resident's Dairy Queen theory. "I suppose there's lots of individual reasons for Killmerites reacting as they do," explained Arnold Born. "It's probably individual convenience, as much as anything"—meaning that they wanted the ease of their children walking to a school just down the street, rather than the discomfort of their children being bused out of town. "That's a general trend in America," Born continued. "We want things now and at our fingertips. A friend of mine runs a Dairy Queen. He says people don't care about the quality. They just don't want to wait." Thus, Born suggests that a convenient second-rate school inside Killmer was preferable to a first-rate one outside.

If these and other explanations help to account for Killmer's behavior, as I believe they do, they nevertheless fail to do justice to the fact that each crisis in Unit 110 is always just the latest in a series wherein Killmer counters a "threatening" school board decision with a movement to secede. In each successive secession attempt different persons have been involved. Thus it is not a set group of people with a bad habit of fostering secession that emerges on each threatening occasion. Certainly there is more going in Killmer and in Unit 110 than can be explained by habit, pride, contentiousness, convenience, or good leadership.

In an attempt to analyze just what it is that is going on there—why the forces that bind Unit 110 together are so flawed in Killmer's case—I shall take a closer look at the community in the light of seven key concepts: *boundaries, integrity,* the *community school, consolidation and centralization, loss,* and *secession.*[1] Like all communities, Killmer has boundaries, boundaries that define where Killmer ends and where other places, with other interests, needs, and valued objects, begin. Killmer's boundaries enclose a place that is characterized by integrity. The community school, for a variety of reasons, is a critical part of this integrity, and it is the existence of integrity in Killmer that differentiates the village from other places, both inside and outside Unit 110, which put up no fight against school consolidation. Consolidation and centralization are school policies that transgress Killmer's boundaries and jeopardize its integrity by threatening to remove its community school. In response, Killmer experiences grief of the sort one feels when faced with the loss of something that provides meaning to one's life. And Killmer reacts to this loss by attempting secession, a defensive effort intended to preserve its integrity.

Boundaries and Integrity

He will not go beyond his father's saying,
And he likes having thought of it so well
He says again, "Good fences make good neighbors."
    —Robert Frost, "Mending Wall"

Over the years, classroom-related issues have animated students and parents, but the controversies of Unit 110, the disputes that mark its imperfection, have not centered on academic matters. The underlying and abiding concern seems strikingly to be not what happens to the children in school but where the children go to school. This does not mean that most parents ignore the academic experience, reserving their ardor

exclusively for the issues of whether their children ride a bus
and where they ride it to. It does mean that from the beginning
I was alerted to boundaries and what they contained, to the
sentiments of persons inside them toward outsiders, and to
persons who responded to this often grim and solemn business
of boundaries with the irritation people reserve for problems
rooted in premises they can hardly believe exist, let alone find
comprehensible. We would hear district residents say, in a tone
of mixed annoyance and surprise, "Don't they want better
education for their kids?" "If they worried as much about their
kids as about their Main Street . . ." And so on, and so on.
"They," the Killmerites, acted as though the political boundary
that set them apart from other villages were a wall. Within this
"wall" were goods worth guarding and transmitting to their
children. Thus, they felt obliged to concern themselves about
where their children's school was located. For the time being,
what happened to their children in school was secondary and
thus could be minimized.

Boundaries of different sorts structure the lives of Unit
110's residents. Many enclose valued entities that inspire little
emotion, like those which define the limits of their water and
telephone services; some are identified as straightforward lines
of convenience drawn on a map, like those which establish the
reach of local ambulance or fire-department service; others
enter their lives intermittently, like those which locate their
polling places. These instances of formal, imposed boundaries
contrast with informal (and therefore much less predictable)
ones which may be altered by mere whim or by chance. Such
are the zones within which residents satisfy personal needs
such as those relating to food, medical care, religion, and
recreation.

Notwithstanding the ostensible commonality of things contained within village boundaries, even the most cursory inspection reveals important distinctions among them. Villages
differ in their makeup, with regard to ethnicity, religions, occupations, social classes, and other factors. They have different
histories, which support different ranges of possible behavior,
and different leadership structures, which permit different

actions from within a number of choices. And they enclose different circumstances and objects. We cannot equate Tipton's and Oldham's dead business sections with Killmer's and Eaton's still live but struggling Main Streets, or Eaton's orderly single-family dwellings with Crandall's trailer park and modestly constructed duplexes.

Less apparent from simple inspection, and far more significant, is another distinction found among villages (or among any groups, for that matter)—their integrity. This attribute is defined by Webster (in the *Third International Dictionary*) as "the quality or state of being complete or undivided: material, spiritual, or aesthetic wholeness: organic unity." Completeness, wholeness, unity—these are the characteristics of integrity that make the term so appropriate in describing a village.

Integrity is not a consequence of size or the intactness of a village's business section; otherwise Crandall would possess it in abundance. In the case of communities, it relates more to a spiritual completeness that can be inferred from a community's response to problems, and even from what the village may define as a problem. The existence of integrity can be inferred from a community's response to threats to its status quo—not necessarily from the wisdom or farsightedness of the response, but simply from its capacity to mount and sustain a response. The community with integrity is sensitive to threats because it is concerned with survival; conscious of its boundaries, it is alive to guarding what is inside them and to monitoring what impinges upon them from the outside; it has a we-they feeling; and it is alert to the consequences of incongruity between itself and other communities, groups, and events. Given integrity, a community's boundaries are sensitive demarcations. Many different acts of passing over them may be seen as trespass, an alien breaching of the barriers. Integrity, like other virtues, is not a matter of all or none, of either having it or not having it. It can increase and decrease, be gained and lost. On a continuum of integrity, Killmer and Eaton would be at the higher end and Tipton and Oldham at the lower end. The evidence on Crandall is uncertain: during the recent events involving Unit 110 it was very slow to act, finally did, and may or may not act again.

Paul Deising's concept (1962) of "social rationality" helps to explicate the notion of integrity; it points up further differences among the villages composing Unit 110 and between the villages and the unit itself. Social rationality, says Deising, "exists when people engage in joint action, when they share experience and understand one another" (236). The residents of Killmer and Eaton demonstrated they could sustain joint action both alone and with each other. On routine matters, Unit 110 regularly engages in joint action via its school board operations, but for years the various villages, as partners in an educational enterprise, have failed to "share experience and understand one another" to a degree sufficient to allow the district to resolve its critical issues. In fact, social rationality and integrity appear to be positively correlated qualities, so that as one increases in magnitude, the other increases also. Neither is a signal attribute of Unit 110. Deising continues: "The parts of an interdependent system fit together and complete each other. . . . The people involved in such a system must each have the same cognitive map of the system, since divergences in maps would lead to conflict or separation in action" (237). Once again, at least as regards school affairs, Killmer acts as an interdependent system with the certainty of a shared cognitive map; the absence of such map in Unit 110 is at the core of its conflict.

Unit 110 lacks the solidarity, the understanding, and the shared cognitive map of Deising's social rationality because its five villages have not, to equal or to sufficient degrees, acceded either to an overarching conception of purpose or to its school board's educational sovereignty. Given such sovereignty, the board could establish goals where there were none or could fulfill them if they existed. Though nominally joined in a union, Eaton and Killmer usually complied with that union's dictates only insofar as they did not endanger their K–8 school. A fixation with a K–8 school, and all that it connotes, has precluded their absorption in the school district; their involvement in it always has been guarded, tentative, and incomplete (with a consequent impairment of Unit 110's integrity). As John Furnivall said of plural societies, Unit 110 "is in the strictest sense a medley, for they [here the villages] mix but do not combine. Each group holds by . . . its own ideas and ways" (quoted in Busch 1974: 123). Furnivall's statement exaggerates the distinctiveness of the school district's villages, but it captures the essence of a disjointed collectivity, one that never adequately coheres for want of an acceptable raison d'être.

The Community School

What is the nature of the school Killmer so arduously defends? More precisely, what does this school mean to the people of Killmer? It means many things, though not all of them are equally important or even important at all to every resident. Of concern to every parent of school-aged children is the school's academic contribution; since the schools in question are elementary schools, their focal point is the three Rs and basic preparation for the compulsory next level of schooling. Eaton residents take special pride in the quality of their school's academic contribution. The school as a place of academic pride may be part of its array of meanings for them. This is not the case in Killmer. Its residents love Killmer Grade School, but the school's academic feats are not and have not usually been worthy of acclaim. This fact alone indicates that something else is going on in regard to their school, that it is not the loss of a good education in their closed school which so animates Killmerites. Furthermore, any school contributes to its society's process of sorting out youth to this or that educational experience or job and, eventually, to this or that status. That schools sort out and do so reasonably effectively does not necessarily endear them to a community; still, as in the case of Eaton's school, if a student's life chances seem to be enhanced by having gone to a certain school, then that school may be noted for this accomplishment.

Beyond these effects, a school enters the lives of members of its host community by means of a set of functions, which may be defined as the status of the school building itself, the school's operational functions, and its symbolic functions.[2] The particulars of this discretely listed but overlapping set are common to, though far from equally important to, schools in all settings. Together they constitute what else is going on in Killmer Grade School.

The School Building

Take the school building itself. It is part of the community's physical landscape; indeed, with very few exceptions, the school has always been present in the lives of living Killmer residents. Thus it belongs to a normal order of things, to a configuration that contains parks, churches, homes, and the like. In this respect, it is not the activities of the school that are important but the place of the building in this comfortable (and comforting) configuration which shapes the physical landscape of Killmer. In addition, the building has a particular meaning for former students. As a graphic reminder of an often hallowed past, it is the physical embodiment of old friendships, old fun, old contests, and, as well, an old self. Certainly, no window-boarded, shut-down school can compete with a still vital school in evoking the life and liveliness of the unabandoned pasts of its many graduates who drive past it, tread its halls as parents, or are touched by it as their children come home with stories out of its ongoing present. Describing another setting, Peter Marris (1974: 55) writes: "The corner shops, the shabby streets, the yards and lots where they played as children are invested with all kinds of intimate associations. They identify with the neighborhood: it is part of them." In like manner, Killmer's school building is invested with "intimate associations," and "it is part of them."

The School's Operational Functions

Other meanings of a school arise from its particular contemporary functions. For example, depending on such factors as the degree of local control, how long its educators have worked there, and the involvement of parents, a school may operate to reinforce the values and outlook of its host community. Parents value a school whose emphases are congruent with their own. Ray Reinhart, Killmer's leader in secession, values such congruency, but he wants more than this: he insists that the community join the school in its socializing role, believing that this can occur only when children attend a school located in their home village. On more than one public occasion, Reinhart said he did not want someone else's community to educate his children. In so thinking, Reinhart joins those American subgroups which establish private schools to insure the idiosyncratic enculturation of their young and to serve as agents of boundary maintenance between the subgroup and the larger, "hostile" world (Kraybill 1977: 1–6).

Reinhart and many others underlined the school's contribution to a village's economic health, arguing, for example, that where there is an open school, there are children waiting to be picked up. This means parents coming to town and taking advantage of being in town to go shopping. Moreover, property owners are persuaded that a school attracts families with school-aged children and that without a school, families move elsewhere and property values decline. They envision a village with a closed school as a place of childless couples and retired persons, and thus with vacant, hard-to-sell homes that were designed for families with three or four children.

Good roads and ready transport long ago minimized village dependence on locally available recreation; in fact, on any given night, there is a steady stream of cars between Killmer and Pageville. Nonetheless, the school's activities form the major part of Killmer's limited recreational opportunities and are of special importance to the elderly. The more grades the local school has, the more activities it generates for community recreation.

The school's activities—the Thanksgiving assembly, the Christmas program, the athletic contests, the awards banquet, etc.—are incorporated in the community's calendar. They help to shape its annual round and also to create a feeling of liveliness in the village. In small places, where there is so little else happening of a public nature, the presence of a school is likely to make a day seem noteworthy, when otherwise days may run unremarkably together, one much like another. Thanks to their school, villagers are afforded something to remark upon that is solely theirs, beginning and ending within their boundaries, of no moment alongside the events of the larger social settings that engulf them, but comfortably theirs. A school's events are internal markers and manifestations of the collective life of the community, witness to a community that to some extent can call its own tune. Enduring as they may be in physical terms, villages and small towns are still sensitive to psychological indicators which bear on their possible health or decline.

Another consequence of these activities, when tied to the accomplishments of individual students and of a school's teams, is the development of pride in *our* students, *our* teams, *our* school. Such collective pride has the potential of attaching people to each other and to the place—Killmer or Eaton— where the activities occur, of creating a feeling of defensiveness when one's place of pride is attacked in some way, and of making one feel good about being from, and identified with, that place. A school is a widely accepted object of loyalty.

The greater number of teams and organizations that exist when there are several open community schools, as opposed to the fewer that exist in a single centralized school, increases the chances of student participation. Killmer and Eaton parents cherish such participation, believing its opportunities for the development of a range of skills is a critical part of the schooling experience. The psychologists Roger Barker and Paul Gump (1964: 202) strongly endorse this view:

> Our findings and our theory posit a negative relationship between school size and individual student participation. . . . What size should a school be? The data of this research and our own educational values tell us that a school should be sufficiently small that all of its students are needed for all of its enterprises. A school should be small enough that its students are not redundant.

Organizational and team activities are a signal dimension of American schools. In fact, parents may be more sensitive to changes in these activities than to changes in academic activities.

The School's Symbolic Functions

And still there is more, for the school serves as a symbol of various sorts.[3]

Community autonomy. The trend of modern society is toward diminishing prerogatives for individuals and their small towns. A school symbolizes community autonomy because of what remains in most states of local control. This point is more hypothetical than real in Killmer. In the case of schools in Unit 110, some degree of local (i.e., village) control prevails, but most of it is in school board hands and thus outside all five communities. The authority the school board has is that which all villages relinquished upon joining Unit 110. But the impression of autonomy somehow remains intact in Killmer.

Community vitality. Viable villages generally contain schools; dying and dead ones either lack them or do not have them for long. The capacity to maintain a school is a continuing indicator of a community's well-being. In the same vein, a community school helps a village feel it is not redundant. Rather, it serves its citizens in several valued ways.

Community integration. Because it is the most inclusive of all community institutions, requiring nothing more for affiliation than that one be a resident, the school is potentially everyone's; all may feel it is theirs. And because of the school's many activities, because valued persons (one's children) attend it, and because of the attributes listed above, the school is frequently a village's most central institution. People are drawn to a school, it gives them something of importance in common, and thus it functions to integrate a community.

Personal control. When the school is down the street, parents feel they can be instrumental in what happens to their children, in physical, moral, and intellectual terms. The school's physical proximity, particularly if it precludes busing, creates the impression of security and safety; distance creates the impression of inaccessibility, if not powerlessness, and of possible contact with strangers.

Personal and community tradition. School tradition embraces not just the building and not just what happens in the building, but also the children walking to and from school, the hubbub of their after-school and weekend playground games, and the expectant silence of the building as August heat ushers in the summer's end and Main Street stores sport their return-to-school signs and sales. The list could grow long, but the point is that the totality of a school assumes its place in tradition, and tradition colors and enriches our individual and collective lives.

Personal and community identity. This aspect of the symbolic dimensions of the school is perhaps the sum total of all previously mentioned ones. The answer to the questions "Who am I?" and "What is this community?" derives, at least in part, from the impact of the school's building and of its operational and symbolic functions on individuals and on the collectivity of individuals who constitute a community. It does not seem farfetched to suggest that in the complex of elements that contribute to personal and community identity, the school has a highly important place.

The schools I characterize here are not the schools of everywhere. They exist in stable urban neighborhoods and in towns possessing a sense of community, but most notably in small, homogeneous places (though not necessarily in all small places, as Tipton and Oldham make clear), where the course of change typically has led to closed shops and diminished autonomy, and has conveyed the impression that what remains is only marginally good, and that what is truly good resides in mass society. Since a school often is a survivor of a village's grander past, it may inspire tenacious possessiveness; high hopes and considerable affect may be attached to it. While the nature of these hopes and the sources of the affect may differ among natives, oldtimers, and newcomers, as well as among parents, businessmen, and widows, such variations cannot obscure the fact that the residents of Killmer and Eaton value their schools highly, and, moreover, that they actively invest value in them and receive, to their way of thinking, substantial returns (note the multiple functions above).

The place of a school in a village's life, and the danger in contemporary affairs both to such schools and to a village's way of life, is admirably developed in Stephen Spender's (1979) summary of the theme in David Jones's book *The Dying Gaul*. Neither Spender nor Jones are writing about schools, but they might as well have been.

> Running through all the essays . . . is an obsessive idea . . . that civilization always threatens and often destroys cultures. Culture is local: the relationship of people living in a given place to the religion they believe in, to the objects that surround them and to one another. Civilization is urban, central and centralizing, and much human history consists of the urban centralizing forces imposing themselves on the local ones and overwhelming them. [9]

And the place of the school in an individual's life is suggested by Anselm Strauss's characterization of possessions.

> "To possess" connotes "to have," but the possession of objects means much more than merely having them around. Self-regard is linked with what is owned, with what is one's own. . . . A problematic world implies the continual danger of losing hold of objects into which great investments have been poured, objects with which we have been heavily involved. [1959: 36–37]

A Killmer resident meaningfully refers to "my school," denoting a possessiveness that results from one, several, or all of the following: having attended the school as a student; being a taxpayer; having a child in the school; and having experienced the school in terms of the range of its functional consequences. One Killmer parent was irate when, after Killmer Grade School was closed, certain materials were moved to another school in the district. Since these materials had been bought by the local student council, she thought they belonged to Killmer. In Strauss's sense, Killmer's school is among Killmer's prized possessions. For years, Unit 110 has represented a "problematic world" in which its school—prized and incorporated as a component of its integrity—was not secure. In Killmer's view, school board policies have repeatedly penetrated Killmer's boundaries and jeopardized its school and, consequently, its community. How staunchly Killmer resists this penetration provides a measure of its integrity.

Consolidation and Centralization

I think Ray Reinhart and the legion of local defenders of the "community school" (that is, a school that is located in the physical and psychological community in which its students live) would be heartened by Spender's words. They esteem the "culture" of their village and the place of their school in this "culture." The proconsolidation school board members are not similarly tied to such settings and thus relate to the schools in Unit 110, including those in the villages nearest them and where they attended school, in an entirely different way. Because of the differences between these two groups, they do not see the acts of consolidation and centralization in the same way.

The essential fact of consolidation is that at least one school in a multischool district is closed and the children from the closed school are usually required to attend a school located outside their own community or neighborhood. The essential fact of centralization is the locating of all or part of a school system in a central site. Centralization invariably involves some degree of consolidation; the converse is not true. Specifically, as Unit 110's recent events affected Killmer and Eaton, these acts of the school board left Killmer without any community school for the first time since its early days before the Civil War and left Eaton with a vastly expanded K–6 school and no junior high school for the first time since 1958.

Though far from new to American education in general, consolidation and centralization are innovations for any particular school district. They clearly involve changes of a nontrivial nature, in that they affect a community by closing its school and affect a group of children by necessitating their accommodation to new children, new teachers, new physical settings, and, possibly, new routines, procedures, and expectations. But unless parents strongly agitate to prevent their children from coming to terms with this new school, children seem quite soon to adjust to it, if not to prefer it. We cannot be equally sanguine about the capacity of a village to adjust to the loss of its school. Of course, the consolidation and centralization policies of the present time are primarily recommended not to challenge students with novel circumstances or to diminish the vitality of village life, but to save money. They are the policies of school districts determined to solve their financial problems.

Unit 110's school board reasoned, "We're in trouble. Consolidation and centralization are constructive steps toward a solution." Killmer and Eaton, on the contrary, interpreted these policies as acts of aggression, as violations of their boundaries and the integrity within. The 1975 announcement of these policies struck West Side residents like a declaration of war, and the results, as in a civil war, promised to be destructive to all contenders. The West Side rejected the rationale behind these policies and focused on their social costs. The ensuing conflict illuminated the different perceptual worlds that characterize both the present turmoil and the district's longstanding cleavage between East and West. Such perceptual contrasts are central to controversies in many realms, as Peter Marris (1974: 56) discusses in reference to a dispute concerning a slum, a dispute that involved redevelopment authorities and residents of the area:

> Each had learned to attach a meaning to [the slum] which the other could not understand. To one it was an anomaly, to the other an integral part of their lives. Neither could revise their conception without radically reconstructing the assumptions on which their purposes and expectations were based.

The incapacity of Unit 110's contenders to revise their conceptions meant the perpetuation of a conflict-ridden status quo.

Loss

In the most direct terms, the policies of consolidation and centralization signify loss—the loss of a school and, therefore, the loss of the functions associated with a village's community school. The KCC protesters, however, characterized the source of their animus not as *losses* (the designation used throughout the discussion that follows) but as *blows*—to their children's physical well-being (busing is unsafe), morality (Crandall is a sinful place), or psychological development (a child is just a number in a large school); and to their community's economic base (Main Street shops will close), integrative capacity (the school holds us together), or simple survival (close our school and you kill our town). For any particular West Side protester, one, several, or all of these purported blows served to motivate protest.

Throughout the four-year period that began in the 1975–76 school year, when the board adopted these policies, the losses or grief attending a closed school were anticipatory[4] for one year (1975–76), when the school was still open; actual for a second year (1976–77), when Killmer Grade School was closed; and merely speculative for two more years (1977–79), when the school was reopened, and not so much as a rumor hinted at the likelihood of its reclosing. During the latter two years, Killmer continued its secession campaign, though it seemed to lack any justification for doing so. Or did it? In this light, the behavior of the KCC seems curious indeed, but I believe the concept of loss will help to clarify their behavior.

To begin with, what was perceived to be "lost" was not precisely the same for each protester; for example, some persons, notably parents of young children, focused on the loss of safety, while others, particularly natives, focused on the loss of community. The list of motivating losses may be ranked in a hierarchy of concern, so that some persons (those for whom the school was a symbol of personal identity) would act as though they had more at stake than others (those for whom upholding real estate values was predominant). I also believe that as a result of intense, prolonged, and anguished discussion over time, those who were moved at first by a single loss eventually endorsed as valid those of their friends and neighbors. Most detachment supporters soon had a set of losses to buttress their own initial sense of what they had been deprived of when their community school was closed. Moreover, individual grief was transformed into collective grief through the Killmer Concerned Citizens's concentration on a single goal—to reopen and keep open the community's grade school. It was of no consequence that the Killmerites attached varying priorities to their different grounds for protest; the critical fact is that their priorities did not engender contradictory sentiments or solutions. Everyone was angry at the same decision (the closing of their school), and their anger was exacerbated by the fact that the decision was made by outsiders (Unit 110's school board); moreover, the same act (reopening the school) would resolve the distress underlying each different sense of loss.

The collective sense of loss generated by Killmer's closed school evoked a reaction comparable to the loss of a beloved family member, in that "once the predictability of events has been invalidated, . . . life will be unmanageable until the continuity of meaning can be restored" (Marris 1974: 41). For Killmerites, the closing of their school disrupted "the predictability of events" and, behaving as though life was unmanageable, they set forth to recover and insure its "continuity of meaning" by a course of secession. To be sure, Killmer's intense, collective response did not arise full-blown immediately after the school board's decision, and not all residents who supported the detachment movement participated to the same extent in that response. The movement, however, eventually subsumed their variant individual reactions and resulted in a generally shared perception of the magnitude of what was at stake in a closed school. I infer this from the overwhelming support to detach evidenced by the requisite two-thirds of the legal voters signing two different detachment petitions (the first one was dismissed as invalid) within a short span of time, by the very large voter turnout for school board elections, and by the success of money-raising efforts, extending over years of protest, by a village possessing only modest economic means.

Marris again points the way to understanding a closed school by designating objects as "structures of meaning." Thus, to lose a community school is not merely to be bereft of a building or a program, but to be deprived of an object that helps make sense of one's life:

> I am concerned with the organized structures of understanding and attachments, by which grown people interpret and assimilate their environment. I have called these "structures of meaning," because in everyday language "meaning" can include a sense of attachment as well as understanding, as when we say something "means a great deal" to someone. [4]

Given a threat to one's structure of meaning, one's conservative impulses are aroused to head off the likely disruption and unpredictability that follow the loss of "a meaningful environment [person, school, etc.] without any change of purpose" (22) regarding that environment.

As we saw in the behavior of the few Killmer and the many non-Killmer residents who accepted consolidation, school loss does not elicit a single, predictable reaction in all those affected by it. Leaving aside the apathetic and the indifferent, the accepters never learned commitment to a community school, even though many grew up in places like Killmer and attended such a school; or if they had learned to be committed, they later acquired overriding commitments which gave them other priorities.

We can begin to explain the positive or negative reaction of Unit 110 residents to what is ostensibly the same event—a closed school—by noting the integrity of their place of residence. It is necessary, in addition, to know how their school is joined to its host community. Of course, each school is embedded in a community, but not in precisely the same way. If Tipton's school, for example, once signified a structure of meaning comparable to Killmer's, it no longer does. As Tipton's population declined and its businesses shut down, its integrity was vitiated. Superficially, Tipton Grade School looks like any other in Unit 110, but for most residents it does not carry the symbolic load of Killmer's grade school. I infer this from the fact that when Tipton's school was closed, Tipton residents accepted with relative ease some other village's school for their children. Their displeasure took the form of grumbling rather than of concerted action of the sort one would expect if the loss of the school was in fact a loss of great consequence. For Tipton residents, the school entailed its conventional, narrower, three-Rs purpose. When this is what is chiefly expected of a school, then, within reason, one school may be as acceptable as any other. Tipton residents accepted the school board's decision to send their children to Oldham's grade school because adequate instruction in the three Rs is a nonexclusive, substitutable function obtainable almost anywhere. Such a decision is unthinkable when, as in Killmer, the school bears a host of idiosyncratic operational and symbolic expectations which can be fulfilled only by a community school peculiar to Killmer.

Not only are different types of communities involved in the reaction to consolidation and centralization, but, I believe, different types of people, as well. At one time I thought these types were associated with certain statuses. For example, the school board decision to consolidate resulted from the vote of five board members, four of whom were farm owners, native to Unit 110, who grew up in its countryside area. By school-district standards, all were prosperous and exceptionally conscious of the farmer's special financial burden for school support; since they not only grew up in the country but also remained there, they and their children are accustomed to busing. Yet many persons possessing none of these characteristics joined them in support of consolidation, while others, farmers like themselves, but from Killmer or Eaton Township, did not. Teachers might have been expected to favor consolidation because it promised greater academic opportunity, but often they split into one camp or the other, depending on their residence on the East or West Side or in Pageville. The proconsolidators were about as heterogeneous as the anticonsolidators who, at first glance, were nonfarming, native, village residents, less well-to-do than the school board's farmers. Further observations turned up newcomers, farmers, and both richer and poorer persons of various occupations.

If I cannot associate distinctive background factors with the anti- and the proconsolidation groups, I do suggest that each group appears to share a cluster of feelings about change and about size; while the clusters are far from pure, they tend to hold up as central tendencies of each group. This impression is derived from my interviews with leaders in Unit 110's conflict and with rank-and-file adults living in the district's townships.

For example, the proconsolidators envisioned the larger school that results from consolidation and centralization as both cost effective and a place of welcome changes where their children would meet a greater variety of other children, where teachers can concentrate on teaching subjects in which they have been specially trained, where greater numbers of students will facilitate grouping students for enhanced instruction, and where higher levels of academic expectation can help prepare children to succeed in a competitive world. While they did not seem to believe that villages themselves would benefit from the loss of a school, their attention—directed to the promise of change—clearly was not riveted to the consequences for a village of closing its school.

That there are many rural persons who welcome change belies the conclusion that they are generally disposed to resist it. There are exemplars of this conservative disposition like Nancy Franklin, KCC executive committee member. She captures the conservative spirit in a terse, poignant expression: "I have my roots deep. I have never liked new situations." And this is what motivated her to face month after month of adversity that would have compelled most persons to slip into accepting the change that required such excessive effort to resist.

Behavior which from a conservative perspective appears endearing and virtuous is from a progressive perspective stodgy and anachronistic. Eaton's and Killmer's minority of antisecessionists joined many East Side residents to condemn the pro–community-school mentality which values modern agriculture but distrusts modern education, which touts the basics but omits science as a basic subject, which lauds intimacy but ignores the curricular limits imposed by the small numbers that enable intimacy, which looks inward at what we have but not outward at what we do not have ("Pageville has more programs than we do; all they talk about here [in Unit 110] is the three Rs, which is good, but not good enough today"); and which holds fast to the anchors of the familiar but overlooks the changing tide.

In regard to change, listen to Julie Pinfield, Crandall resident and teacher:

> If you look out in every direction from my house, you can see where the little country schools used to be. They no longer exist. Many people were very disturbed when they closed, but the earth didn't stop and we recovered. Maybe this is another time when we have to face yet another change. Social change is never easy.

Pinfield refers here to the wave of consolidation which gave birth to Unit 110s all over the state and virtually wiped out the one-room country school. I suspect she is generally right in thinking that what exists and you cannot make go away, you eventually get reconciled to, though she may underestimate the potential resistance to changes which entail ever increasing scale. For some persons, the preference and the tradeoff are clear: "If it takes consolidation to get a better education, then I say let's do it. Of course, I'd like to have a school in town, but not if the price is a poorer education." For others, almost any price paid to send children to larger schools in larger communities is excessive. They fear the loss of intimacy and control that attend such changes and, unlike Julie Pinfield, act as though the earth will indeed stop and that they will never recover if such changes occur.

Pinfield was prepared to take change in stride, accepting its inevitability and, to her and to others like her, its opportunities. Not so the anticonsolidators. They abhorred both the location and the increased size of consolidated and centralized schools, believing that their out-of-community location would entail the losses noted above. They also believed that increased size would introduce greater and undesirable (1) heterogeneity, and thus a greater probability of "unacceptable" children interacting with their own; (2) anonymity, and thus a greater probability their children may become faceless figures, mere ciphers lost in a big education mill; (3) powerlessness and incomprehensibility for both themselves and their children, since the large school is more complex and thus more difficult to comprehend and to control; (4) formality, in the conventional way that increased size, whether of government, corporations, or schools, seems always to require more rules and more rigid enforcement of regulations; and (5) pace, as the slower, more leisurely ways of a smaller setting give way in a larger one to accentuated preoccupation with time, deadlines, and getting things done.

Groups holding varying opinions on the dimensions of change and size have been labeled traditional or modern, conservative or progressive, parochial or cosmopolitan. These labels refer to stereotypes, whereas the real people in Unit 110 actually hold a confusing amalgam of values, values that are often situational in their application. For example, when one of the school district's consolidators faced the threat of a distant church hierarchy closing his village church (the consolidation and centralization of churches results from the same forces that affect schools), he led the opposition to this decision with arguments plucked shamelessly from Killmer's script. Was he unprincipled? No, he just did not see the school and the church in the same light: each touched his life in a different way, and he could apply a different rationale to each one. Viva compartmentalization! Moreover, in Marris's view, although this man had acquired a commitment to his community church which made it a structure of meaning in his life, he had not acquired a comparable commitment to his community school.

Finally, the anti- and the proconsolidators diverged on the nature of academic quality. The matter of quality education had been emphasized long before, in the 1948 document that created Unit 110. Interestingly, it urged school districts to be "satisfactory channels for good education as well as of local control." Of course, the words could be dismissed as a mere rhetorical flourish. I choose, rather, to see them as reflecting an unexamined dilemma which underlay the work of the 1948 school survey committee and which remained manifest for thirty years: although school districts were to be "satisfactory channels for good education," they were at the same time to be "good instruments for local control." Yet local control, if it means anything, certainly should not mean that villages become ghost towns. Even granting that the causal relationship here is debatable, we still do not know what educational outcomes the school survey committee imagined would remain for local communities to control after reorganization had taken place. The writers of the words in question bowed to the hallowed concept of local control without acknowledging that by ushering in reorganization they had divested the term of much meaning for communities like the villages of Unit 110. As for "good education"—in whose terms? Are they those of the local community, as implied by "local control," those of the school child, or possibly, those of the nation as a whole? In some settings, all three may be equally well served by the same "good" education. But in rural areas good education may have strikingly different meanings for cosmopolitan professionals and for local opinion-makers like Killmer's editor Glenn Davids, for whom things "were going along in fine shape until this reorganization popped up." Davids and others like him never acted as though they believed schools were (as the *Pageville Press* had it) "for the benefit of the children who attend them, rather than for the benefit of the adults who control them." Davids would have been right to reject the claim: the statement confuses the immediate, individual target of schooling—the immature student—with the ultimate, collective reason for schooling the immature—the well-being of society. Unclarified, "good education" and "local control" may be mutually contradictory concepts; certainly, their antithetical consequences plagued Unit 110.

Over the years, the proconsolidators acclaimed academic learning of high quality as the primary end of schooling (though they would readily admit that social and other benefits flowed from it). They scolded the anticonsolidators on this point, accusing them of preoccupation with community rather than with children. Academic quality proved to be a thorny issue for the anti- group. No, they were not unmindful of its importance; yes, they thought their schools could be improved. But they defined the academic issue not as one of enhancing quality but as one of eliminating frills. They were content with what they thought was an "adequate" education for their children, resisting as debatable or illusory what others called the "best" education. Perhaps in other circumstances they would have felt otherwise. Given their view of what was at stake, however, they staunchly resisted arguments for organizational change couched in the language of enhanced academic opportunity. If the argument was joined at the point of political control for a Glenn Davids, it was joined at the point of social control for the KCC's Ned Ruback. He demonstrates his interest in the quality of his daughter's education by his distress over her succession of first-year teachers. Yet he does not infer from the results in Eaton, during the year Killmer's school was closed and when teachers could readily sort out the academically stronger Eaton children from the academically weaker Killmer children, that Killmer's children would have been better off staying in Eaton Grade School. When asked about the supposed benefits of a larger school, he quickly dismissed them—"You just don't gain that much"—preferring to concentrate on the social problems attending an increase in size.

Furthermore, the anticonsolidators (with one notable exception) were mostly back-to-the-basics advocates who felt that when the schools returned to their traditional mission, they would be on the right path. And yet they would grow uneasy at the repeated accusation that they were, in effect, academic know-nothings. The anticonsolidators stated well their specific worries—busing is dangerous or a closed school means less business in town. But, lacking experience in articulating the broadly considered case of the losses connoted by a closed school, they struggled and failed to establish a place for educational quality in the overall context of their communal and personal concerns. Killmer residents demonstrated (by demanding the removal of their children from the academically superior Eaton Grade School) that they would accept the lesser quality of their own school in order to reap the gains they attributed to having it open and operational.

The exception referred to above is that energetic, vital couple who served on the KCC executive committee—Mary and Alf Reeder. They thought the school board had no basis for closing Killmer's school and that Eaton Grade School with Killmer children in it was too crowded to be safe, but they stated their fundamental case for secession in academic terms. Their comparative study of the curriculum in Unit 110 and in Garrison, the school district which Killmer hoped to join, persuaded them that Garrison's was superior. To the Reeders, Garrison meant a chance to gain both quality education and a community school. Anselm Strauss reasons that "if in large measure [a person] rejects the explanations he once believed, then he has been alienated and lost a world" (1969: 38). The Reeders were angry and ready to secede. Those with deep Killmer roots, like the Reinharts and the Nancy Franklins, also were angry and ready to secede. For the latter, however, it was not the gains of annexation to Garrison but the fears of losing a world that stirred their souls.

Secession

And when people draw the boundaries of where they do not belong, their insecurity will project upon those they exclude menacing and disparaging qualities.
—Peter Marris, *Loss and Change*

Secession is the most extreme act short of violence and civil war that any subpart of a political unit can take against that unit. It is not necessarily a rejection of all that the unit stands for, but it clearly declares that the subpart perceives some aspect of the unit as fundamentally antithetical to the subpart's well-being. The subpart in question is Killmer and its concerned citizens; the unit is Unit 110. To be sure, civil war was unthinkable; violence and destruction were thinkable but not seriously considered. Secession became Killmer's banner; in raising it Killmer also raised a barrier of rejection between itself and the rest of Unit 110. After all, what other interpretation could school-district residents place upon a determined effort to achieve a permanent separation from the district?

By their name, the Killmer Concerned Citizens announced an ordinary fact—that they are citizens of Killmer. And then they informed Killmer, Unit 110, and everyone else that they are not just *any* citizens of Killmer, they are *concerned* ones. This is the extraordinary fact which set them apart from others in Killmer who are citizens but not concerned. At the outset, just how concerned they were and how concerned they would remain was open to question. The answer came soon. Their effective access to public attention left no doubt about the source of their distress and the target of their action. Eventually, "concerned" would seem too tame to characterize some KCC activists, though no other name was as direct and unambiguous. "Distressed," "angry," "aroused," "enraged"— no, these and other alternatives seem not to fit as well. To secure the world they feared to lose, the KCC, disparaging those who threatened their security, directed Killmer toward secession, pursuing it for several years through legal channels from county court to state supreme court. They were determined to leave Unit 110.

Killmerites who signed the detachment petition did so for various reasons. Perhaps many of them signed to protest the school board's decision in the same sense some Europeans were said to have voted Communist—to register an antigovernment protest when alternative means did not seem to be available. I heard people say, "I didn't sign to go to Garrison, but because I think something has to be done." We do not know how many Killmerites signed simply to register their profound dismay at the closing of their school. Perhaps many signers came to believe, as did one Killmer mother, that, "I don't care about education. I just want my kids to go to Garrison." Given the belief that schools have a communal function, we readily understand this mother who did not "care about education." When her child or her school were "jeopardized," she had more urgent things on her mind than arithmetic.

Clearly, parents do not respond to the education of their children in predictable, linear, or obviously rational ways.

The idea of secession is unsettling. Even though the union of five villages and seven townships was not made in heaven, it had, like a marriage, resulted from a solemn joining together; it had endured, had taken on the semblance of an established institution, and had been incorporated into the personal meaning structures of many people; and it was the object of a network of obligations and expectations. The school district was not a ready candidate for dismantling; to divide it by secession was, for many, to violate an established order. Accordingly, if secession offered an attractive solution to Killmer, it was anathema to many others in Unit 110 because of its disruptive potential.

If the threat of secession generates its own opposition, it also has its latent instructive aspects, both negative and positive. We can conjecture that each secession struggle, even if abortive, may serve to make secession a more thinkable alternative until, like divorce, it becomes a relatively commonplace response to a particular set of circumstances. Alternatively, the prospect of secession may so dramatize and illuminate the issues, may so clarify what is at stake for both protagonists and antagonists, that a solution is facilitated. Moreover, even though a secession attempt fails, it may still serve as a safety valve for the overheated tempers of its instigators.

All three of these possible consequences of secession occurred in Unit 110. The harder Killmer tried to secede, the more antagonism it aroused elsewhere in the district. Beyond feeling antagonized, people began to yearn for peace and to consider solutions (which earlier they would have rejected), if the solutions offered any hope of peace. "I've gotten to the point," said an Oldham man, "where even if we lose money it wouldn't bother me if Killmer left. I'm willing to pay a price for peace." Of course, he was not tested to see whether he would actually support increased taxes, but he made at least a large verbal concession, in a school district not noted for its financial generosity, by announcing that he would consider doing so. Here we see one consequence of the secession-

inspired conflict—it eventually reconstructed feelings so
that what was once beyond consideration at length became
thinkable.

In addition, a consensus was emerging; though residents
did not reach unanimity in their outlook, they grouped themselves around several essential understandings. This observation excludes the views of two groups—Killmer's resolute
secessionists, who rejected any tie with Unit 110, and those
non-Killmerites who for different reasons agreed that Unit 110
would be better off if Killmer left the school district. To begin
with, no one doubted that the district faced serious financial
problems. This is a major achievement, because school patrons
cannot seriously consider policy decisions which derive from
the premise of a red budget until they accept that premise. It
is like proposing solutions to an energy crisis when people do
not believe a crisis exists. Given this understanding, residents
took seriously the idea of a referendum to increase property
taxes. Furthermore, the unpredictable decision-making process in the district so dismayed residents that they clamored
at school board meetings for a long-range plan. The board,
however, delighted simply to agree on any plan at all, never
turned to long-range considerations; it focused, instead, on a
plan for the 1977–78 school year. And, finally, though diehard
K–8ers resisted the centralized junior high school and diehard
consolidators resisted any plan but a single K–12 campus, a
clear consensus developed for a community school, preferably
a K–6, in each town.

There were alternatives to secession, but consider the circumstances from the KCC's perspective. For almost three decades, Unit 110 had suffered from an East-West split, a fact
that was fixed in the school district's history as a reminder that
the district harbored strong differences of opinion and policy.
To Killmer, the most drastic school board decision was the one
that completely closed their only school. Surely the board was
hateful and spiteful and acted unjustifiably. A supposedly capricious, destructive board majority and an indecisive, vacil-
lating superintendent, whose authority and capacity to lead
had been undermined by an antagonistic board, could hardly

be less reassuring for Killmer's future. Killmer soon added one more negative characteristic to those they already attributed to the board—untrustworthiness; indeed, this view became widespread in the district. And district residents also confirmed Killmer's belief that the board was incompetent. This overall negative picture cut across villages, groups, and sides; Killmer was encouraged to learn that they were not alone in believing that Unit 110 lacked a "legitimate" authority.

> We may define "legitimacy" to be a moral bond between the citizen and the state: to the degree that this bond exists, most members of the polity see their political institutions as morally proper for their society and they feel there is an obligation to obey the incumbents of those institutions. [Busch 1974: 1]

Killmer reasoned that with the board lacking any bond of legitimacy but having the votes to shut their school, and with Unit 110's school boards and superintendents bent upon consolidation and centralization, then there could be no secure future—of the sort that a community school makes possible—for Killmer in Unit 110. Accordingly, secession was imperative.

For almost four years (1976–79) Unit 110 endured the anomaly of Killmer's detachment efforts. It bore the legal costs of going before regional educational authorities to meet the KCC petition with counterarguments, and it bore the uncertainty of not knowing from year to year what permanence their decisions would have and what resources would be at their disposal for the next school year. The detachment appeal, like a filibuster in the United States Senate, constantly reminded the school district that a minority element was acutely unhappy. Not soon would Unit 110 residents forget about Killmer's attachment to its community school. In addition, Killmer's determination to withdraw exacerbated the districts' already existing we-they feelings, and thereby further etched the boundaries that separated Killmer from Unit 110. The filibuster analogy is particularly appropriate in another sense: it was the fact of Killmer's *permanent* minority status that generated the drive to secede even after they achieved a 5-2 school board majority. Secession, like a filibuster, is a means of managing events perceived as negative which cannot be managed by other political means. Given that Crandall alone was larger than Killmer and Eaton together, Killmer residents concluded that their school board victories could easily prove ephemeral. Thus they sought security through secession. Killmer perceived secession as a conservative policy calculated to perpetuate what it valued, rather than a radical policy designed to disrupt the order of their educational union.

In the Future

Like many a promised land, Garrison seemed tantalizingly close, but it ultimately stayed well beyond Killmer's reach. Now Killmer accepts its status quo; its concerned citizens stopped meeting after an abortive attempt to get the state supreme court to hear its case. Superintendent Hanson, the late Warren Hart's successor, though he applied for and failed to get a job elsewhere, seems to be well accepted throughout the district.[5] No exciting events draw reporters to Unit 110's school board room; the district's media potential seems limited to its successful girls' volleyball team. However, about a month before school opened for the fall 1979 semester, the *Pageville Press* reported Superintendent Hanson's reaction to the school board's decision to disallow, for the second consecutive year, a kindergarten in Tipton.

> "I can see why people don't want their youngsters transported when they are very small," Hanson said. But he added that there had been no real problems involved with busing the Tipton kindergarten students last year, the first time it was done.
> "I have to come through with a recommendation that is the most economically feasible as well as educationally sound. I've thought a lot about it, as I know some of you have," Hanson told the board.
> "I really feel the educational program will be the same whether it's offered at Tipton or Oldham," he said.

By accepting the superintendency in Unit 110, Superintendent Hanson moved into one of the toughest administrative positions in the state; he demonstrated impressive skill and sensitivity in reversing the district's declining financial fortunes and its sliding morale. Yet, when he assures Tipton parents that their youngsters will receive the same education in Oldham as in Tipton, he endorses the same tradition of rationality and efficiency that his predecessors in the superintendent's office and on the school board have espoused. I have no basis for taking issue with his decision in this kindergarten case, but I believe his assurance to Tipton's parents ignores the range of possible meanings that Killmer has demonstrated a school may hold for these and other district parents. In actuality, he may arouse only limited antagonism when such decisions involve Tipton and Oldham. When they involve Killmer and Eaton, they will touch raw nerves. That he could assert this instrumental rationale—"the educational program will remain about the same"—so soon after Killmer's tempestuous secession struggle, raises doubts about whether anyone in authority in Unit 110 has truly learned anything at all from its recent storm.

Perhaps the one, clear, fundamental good that has come out of the conflict of these past several years is a substantially enhanced, cross-village awareness of the desire to keep children in village-based schools and of the very special place such schools have in the communities of Killmer and Eaton. It is still too soon, however, to tell how deeply this awareness has penetrated and how enduring its impact will be, since one thing is unequivocally clear: in the several years of recent controversy, the community school did not assume new functions; it did not become something it had never been before. Its ascension to the pantheon of mom and apple pie was the result not of something novel and useful it had just begun to do, but of the illuminating experience occasioned by Killmer's dogged desire to secede. The community school was uncovered, not created. School-district residents became conscious of the significance of the local school in their community life.

Notwithstanding the community school's explicit enshrinement in the latest school board policy, we may doubt that its antagonists are demolished. Rather, they may be lying dormant until the next financial pinch stimulates a search for cost-saving measures. Listen to Jerry Townsend of Oldham and Steve Shear of Eaton, each of whom represents a certain outlook:

> I really don't know why Killmer squeaks so loud. I think basically all the towns are made up of the same kind of people.

> They're all the same color. Difference in religion doesn't enter into it at all. I really can't say why one town feels so differently about consolidation.

In short, if we are all alike, then how can we understand or justify the behavior of some group (Killmer) that assumes it's different and acts as if it really were? In Jerry Townsend's limited grasp of what makes Killmer run lies the seed of future Unit 110 disorder. Steve Shear adds another dimension:

> It's terrible to think, but the ones who are making the biggest fuss are not thinking about quality of education. They're thinking solely about community. We have a conflict. If it has to happen, we should maintain quality of education at the expense of community. The school is a great local center. It is worth preserving if we can afford it.

Unlike Townsend, Shear understands what motivates Killmer, and if forced to make a choice he would choose education. Drawn together from different starting points, Townsend and Shear are potential allies for consolidation. They would be joined by a third, large, ubiquitous group—the one that invariably places finances ahead of all other considerations and makes decisions accordingly.

Since the attractions of consolidation are not yet part of Unit 110's inert past, Killmer would be well-advised not to dismantle its barricades.[6] Killmer may have builders of barricades as long as it has some critical mass of "people who have never left and grow up not knowing what it's like in other places. There are always these roots. It's hard to see faults when you've lived somewhere all your life." And it may be hard to see virtues when you've not! It is not, however, the natives alone who constitute the backbone of the KCC; it is also the newcomers who moved to Killmer to get away from Pageville's so-called urban disorder, and were startled to find that Killmer and Unit 110 h‌‍ ‍ disorder of its very own.

Past imperfections of   ‍ 110's educational union stemmed from the clash of priorities about school and community. At present, barring the erosion of Killmer's integrity, and a consequently changed Killmer, the only basis for a less imperfect union lies in the school district's accepting a commitment to perpetuate community schools wherever they are until enrollment declines and financial pressures make them indisputably unthinkable.

At times, after repeated long nights of interviews and meetings that had been preceded by months of the same, I would remember that somewhere in this turmoil the routines of schooling prevailed; somewhere, teachers and students worked and played in classrooms, assembly halls, gyms, and corridors. How wonderful the mundane can seem when juxtaposed with the excitement of conflict! The drama of Unit 110 evolved with scant regard for its routines, though its contentious actors would, if challenged, glibly relate that what they did was meant to have a positive impact on the students' daily school life, and, of course, on their future. If Senator Black was right in thinking that the "local man" is passing, the ruckus in Unit 110 testifies to the fact that he has not yet fully passed away. But consider this statement, so distant from the perspective of the local man's community school:

> "There is a quality of life which lies beyond the mere fact of life." The great teacher is he who can convey this sense of quality to another, so that it haunts his every endeavor. . . . It is education that provides that touch of eternity under the aspect of which endurance can pass into dignified, wry acceptance, and animal enjoyment into a quality of living. [Peters 1965: 112]

And consider this statement, with its perspective so distant from that of the consolidators. A community may be bound up with one's identity such that it

> has become an extension of an inhabitant's ego so that any action which seems to diminish the status of the community and its security becomes, in effect, a threat to the self and security . . . of the individual involved. [Jonassen 1968: 32]

From the insularity of their perceptual fortresses, the advocates of fiscal responsibility, of academic opportunity, and of the community school not only differed in the priorities they assigned to their treasures within, they defined them in ways that the victory of one demanded the defeat of the others. But the fine images in these words of Peters and Jonassen, decidedly too fine to characterize the nature of education in most schools and the nature of community in most villages, forcibly remind us that we ought to attend to the parallel concerns of both school and community, while avoiding equally the trap of believing that what is familiar is good or that what is new is necessarily better.

Epilogue

On June 7, 1980, the *Pageville Press* stretched an article across the bottom of its third page under the heading, "Unit 110 Edges toward Central Campus Idea." The newspaper's staff writer reported his gleanings from a recent school board meeting which featured the recommendations of the Citizens Advisory Council. The council had been meeting for more than a year. Its report, highlighted in the article, "narrowly favored the concept of a single campus for students in kindergarten through 12th grade to replace the district's current network of seven scattered schools." Board members, the article continued, favored the prospect of new construction more than the repair of the existing old buildings.

Sam Nichols, current school board president, was invited to elaborate on the state of affairs in Unit 110:

> The current school board members have much more co-operation with each other than has been the case for a long time. Most of us are good friends. The town rivalry thing that was so strong before is not an immediate problem now. All of us on the board now would vote against their own town if they thought the issue was right. There's nothing in the picture about closing schools in Eaton and Killmer or removing any grades from an existing school. No, not

for the next few years, anyway. I think there's a new mainstream in Killmer that gives no thought of leaving Unit 110 and going to Garrison. Ray Reinhart will never change, but there's others in Killmer."

Ray Reinhart reacted to this particular school board meeting by observing, "We knew all the time they hadn't changed their mind."

Township	1920
	Total
Killmer	1,383
Village	546
Rural	837
Eaton	1,169
Village	544
Rural	625
Crandall	1,410
Village	693
Rural	717
Oldham	1,128
Village	478
Rural	650
Tipton	1,644
Village	413
Rural	1,231
Crawford	727
Browne	704

Appendix

Tables

TABLE 1
Population of Unit 110's Townships, 1920–70

1930		1940		1950		1960		1970	
Total	% Change	Total	% Change	Total	% Change	Total	% Change	Total	% Change
1,306	− 5.6	1,261	− 3.4	1,110	− 12.0	1,125	+ 1.4	1,299	+ 15.5
539	− 1.3	567	+ 5.2	653	+ 15.1	686	+ 5.1	915	+ 33.4
767	− 8.4	694	− 9.5	457	− 34.1	439	− 3.9	384	− 12.5
1,104	− 5.6	1,105	− 9.0	1,021	+ 1.5	1,211	+ 18.6	1,453	+ 20.0
512	− 5.9	510	− 0.4	525	+ 2.9	740	+ 41.0	1,022	+ 38.1
592	− 5.3	495	− 16.4	496	+ 0.2	471	− 5.0	431	− 8.5
1,371	− 2.8	1,366	− 0.4	1,499	+ 9.7	1,903	+ 27.0	2,406	+ 26.4
790	+ 14.0	876	+ 10.9	1,065	− 21.6	1,539	+ 44.5	2,027	+ 31.7
581	− 19.0	490	− 15.7	434	− 11.4	364	− 16.1	379	+ 4.1
988	− 12.4	827	− 16.3	756	− 8.6	765	+ 1.2	789	+ 3.1
404	− 15.6	367	− 9.1	415	+ 13.1	468	+ 12.8	536	+ 14.5
584	− 10.1	460	− 21.2	341	− 25.9	297	− 12.9	253	− 14.8
1,492	− 9.2	1,437	− 3.7	722	− 46.3	693	− 10.2	743	+ 7.2
353	− 14.5	371	− 5.1	388	+ 4.6	384	− 1.0	454	+ 18.2
1,139	− 7.5	1,066	− 6.4	384	− 64.0	309	− 20.8	289	− 6.5
728	+ 0.0	490	− 18.9	205	− 65.2	179	− 13.1	160	− 10.2
599	− 15.0	522	− 12.8	158	− 69.7	143	− 9.8	127	− 11.3

SOURCE: *U.S. Census of Population*.

TABLE 2
Unit 110 Townships: Socioeconomic Profile, 1970

	Killmer	Eaton	Crandall	Oldham	Tipton
Education					
Attended high school	55.4%	62.7%	62.2%	62.2%	60.2%
Attended college	11.7%	12.7%	13.8%	15.5%	10.9%
Marital status					
Divorced persons	1.8%	2.3%	1.5%	0.8%	1.0%
Separated or spouse absent	0.5%	0.0%	0.7%	1.4%	0.9%
Family income					
Median range	$8,000–$9,000	$10,000–$11,000	$10,000–$11,000	$10,000–$11,000	$10,000–$11,000
Under $5,000	21.2%	9.6%	12.3%	13.2%	17.9%
Below poverty level	9.1%	3.6%	3.2%	7.3%	3.9%

SOURCE: *U.S. Census of Population, 1970 (Fourth Count).*

TABLE 3
Enrollments in Township School Systems, 1940–48

Township	1940–41	1941–42	1944–45	1945–46	1946–47	1947–48	1948–49
Killmer							
Grade school	106[a]	88	129	140	127	132	178
High school	70	78	76	61	64	62	64
Eaton							
Grade school	61	50	46	58	61	80	104
High school	57	58	53	57	45	59	59
Crandall							
Grade school	140	138	126	129	151	154	179
High school	79	77	78	77	82	90	101
Oldham							
Grade school	41	36	30	28	25	20	68[b]
High school	36	30	17	18	17	18	0
Tipton							
Grade School	54	46	45	49	54	66	89
High school	103[c]	111	66	65	76	68	60

SOURCE: Unit 110 files.
NOTE: All grade schools contained eight grades and all high schools, four grades.
[a] I do not know why so many fewer students were in the high school as compared with the grade school; perhaps many Killmer children stopped their formal education after the eighth grade.
[b] At least part of the large discrepancy between grade and high school enrollments is due to the presence of a local parochial school. I do not know how much of the discrepancy this fact explains.
[c] Enrollment jumped this year because the local parochial school closed down.

TABLE 4
Unit 110: Students and Employees by Superintendent's Tenure, 1962–78

	No. Students	Certified Employees		Noncertified Employees		Total Employees
		Full-time	Part-time	Full-time	Part-time	
Donald Gaumnitz						
1962	1,521	82	0	25	6	113
1963	1,685	87	2	30	10	129
1964	1,621	88	4	27	16	135
1965	1,621	88	4	27	15	134
1966	1,685	91	5	—[a]	—	—
1967	1,798	96	4	29	16	145
1968	1,860	98	4	43	7	152
Jason Talman						
1969	1,910	105	2	45	7	159
1970	1,904	114	4	49	11	178
1971	1,878	117	3	49	11	180
Warren Hart						
1972	1,901	120	3	46	7	176
1973	1,843	120	3	46	7	176
1974	1,766	125	4	42	4	175
1975	1,773	112	3	40	8	163
1976	1,786	95	0	36	2	133
Burt Hanson						
1977	1,695	98	1	38	2	137
1978	1,623	—	—	—	—	—

SOURCE: Unit 110 files.

NOTE: Certified employees are teachers and administrators; noncertified employees are persons such as custodians, cooks, and secretaries.

[a] Information lacking.

TABLE 5
Unit 110: Receipts and Expenditures by Superintendent's Tenure, 1963–77

Year	Receipts	Expenditures	Difference
		Donald Gaumnitz	
1963	1,270,597	1,185,220	+ 85,337
1964	1,577,963	1,676,466	− 98,503
1965	1,788,889	1,178,624	+610,265
1966	1,276,570	1,235,699	+ 40,871
1967	1,093,359	1,387,176	−293,817
1968	977,336	1,597,181	−619,845
		Jason Talman	
1969	2,438,284	2,003,851	+434,433
1970	2,160,305	2,109,670	+ 50,635
1971	2,075,862	2,755,367	−679,505
		Warren Hart	
1972	2,742,693	2,296,166	+446,527
1973	2,442,811	2,410,457	+ 32,354
1974	2,471,512	2,527,987	− 56,475
1975	2,441,430	3,052,642	−611,212
1976	2,798,006	2,295,965	+502,041
		Burt Hanson	
1977	1,788,957	2,537,819	−748,862
1978	—	—	−477,470

SOURCE: Unit 110 files.

TABLE 6
Shifting Organizational Arrangements in Unit 110 Schools

	Killmer	Eaton	Crandall	Oldham	Tipton
1948–49	K–12	K–12	K–12	K–8	K–12
1949–53	K–9	K–6	K–6	K–6	K–9
			7–8		
			9–12		
1953–58	K–9	K–6	K–4	K–6	K–4
			10–12		7–9
1958–62	K–8	K–8	K–8	K–8	K–8
			9–12		
1962–63	K–8	K–8	K–8	K–6	K–8
			9–12		
1963–75	K–8	K–8	K–3	K–6	K–6
			7–8		
			9–12		
1975–76	K–6	K–8	K–3	K–6	K–6
			7–8		
			9–12		
1976–77	0	K–6	K–2	K–6	3
			7–8		
			9–12		
1977–78	K–6	K–6	K–4	K–6	K–3
			7–8		
			9–12		
1978–79	K–6	K–6	K–4	K–6	1–4
			7–8		
			9–12		

TABLE 7
Results of the Reorganization Referendum in Village Precincts, April 1948

Village	Votes Cast (= N)	For	Against
Killmer	87	44 (51%)	43 (49%)
Eaton	90	75 (83%)	15 (17%)
Crandall	189	154 (82%)	35 (18%)
Oldham	61	57 (93%)	4 (7%)
Tipton	83	25 (30%)	58 (70%)
Total	510	355 (70%)	155 (30%)

SOURCE: School board minutes.

TABLE 8
Voter Response to the School-Building Referendum, November 1970

Township	Votes Cast (= N)	For	Against
Killmer	479	119 (25%)	360 (75%)
Eaton	486	126 (26%)	360 (74%)
Crandall	557	327 (59%)	230 (41%)
Oldham	267	112 (42%)	155 (58%)
Tipton	234	80 (34%)	154 (66%)
Total	2,023	764 (38%)	1,259 (62%)

SOURCE:School district minutes.

Notes

Prologue

1. "Unit 110" is a pseudonym, as are the names of most persons and places referred to in this book. Unit districts are so called because they contain a complete kindergarten-through-twelfth-grade (K–12) system organized under a single school board. Unit 110, organized in 1948, contained five previously independent school systems identified with five politically distinct villages—Killmer, Eaton, Crandall, Oldham, and Tipton—and a host of one-room school districts. The facts presented here and elsewhere in the book are drawn from actual census data, newspaper accounts, etc.; only the names have been changed.

Chapter 1

1. It is the possible relationship between a community's schools and community survival that attracted me to Unit 110 in the first instance. What I had already learned about Killmer encouraged me to think that a study of the conflict there would form a logical sequel to my research on the village of Mansfield (Peshkin 1978).

Chapter 2

1. Davids is mentioned frequently hereafter because at the very inception of Unit 110 he articulated a point of view about the community school that is still shared by Killmer's leaders. And in light

of Killmer's several decisions to secede, I have no doubt that he spoke for the majority of Killmerites in the early years of Unit 110's history. As I became aware of his prominence, I was struck by his similarity to Ben Matthews, editor of Mansfield's village newspaper in *Growing Up American*. Small-town editors often were unusually important in the development and maintenance of their communities.

2. The state school code uses the term "detachment" to characterize the process whereby a part of a school district withdraws from that school district. I prefer the term "secession" because its customary usage in historical and political literature carries with it an emotional tone and a sense of seriousness that fits the case in Unit 110. "Exit" is another term that conveys a basic meaning similar to detachment and secession. It comes from Albert Hirschman's book *Exit, Voice, and Loyalty*. All three terms will be used hereafter.

3. Though located in Pageville, the *Press* means to serve the entire county. Thus one expects to see the paper cover Unit 110 events and to have school-district residents use its pages to disseminate their views.

4. This was an exceptional accomplishment, in that Killmer and Eaton contain persons differentiated by age, occupation, education, income, years of residence in the township, and number of children in school—all factors which, presumably, could affect not only how a person would vote but also whether the person would bother to vote at all. Clearly, the issue of a school's location, and the meanings of its location to those affected, cut across the differences that characterize the various groups composing the community.

5. To my regret, I cannot elaborate Judge Harker's decision. I have not been able to locate the legal record of this hearing, and the newspaper accounts, quite full at the outset of the Elm Place case, were of no help, as the press (and the petitioners as well) had lost interest in the endless legal proceedings.

Chapter 4

1. This is a state administrative unit; its head is the successor to the historic county superintendent of schools.

Chapter 5

1. If an accounting occurs, it involves the financial affairs of an entire school district. Illinois law requires apportioning a district's assets and liabilities with its seceding subpart.

2. Mrs. Coler actually lives in Browne, not Tipton, Township. As mentioned earlier, Browne and Crawford are the two school-district townships which contain very few people and no village at all. For

all practical purposes, Tipton is the effective population area for Coler, as Crandall, rather than Crawford, is for Arlberg. Browne and Crawford become important only at election time when the gentlemen's agreement is invoked and an effort is made to insure that each township has one, but only one, representative.

Chapter 8

1. My analysis will not examine the traditional issues relating to consolidation decisions. These issues include the range of arguments presented to support either closing a school or keeping it open—for example, cost savings, curriculum improvement, and more efficient use of staff, versus busing hazards, declining business and real estate values, and loss of community solidarity. The literature is replete with these contradictory claims (see Sher 1977). A study of these issues would require data from a broad sample of towns and villages and so is beyond the scope of the present work. A study of this sort would be valuable, however, and is long overdue.

2. The list here of a school's attributes or functions is not original with me. Other writers, Gehlen (1969: 26), for example, have referred to them. I see the list as important in the context of understanding a community's response to its closed school.

3. For further discussion of a school's symbolic functions see Bidwell (1965: 1009–10), Alford (1960: 350–71), and Selznick (1957: 5–22).

4. For an elaboration of the concept of anticipatory grief in a psychiatric context see Schoenberg et al. (1974). Aldrich, a contributor to Schoenberg's reader, characterizes anticipatory grief as "any grief occurring prior to a loss" (1974: 4). Arkin, in the same volume, develops a concept of loss that is very much to the point in comprehending the significance of losing a school:

> The cognitive-emotional needs of diverse types are gratified in relationships to other persons, pets, institutions of employment, one's dwelling, and so on. . . . These provide us with something to love dearly. . . . In addition, the components of such relationships become familiar units of individual cognitive maps by which we navigate through our separate worlds and which impart a predictable stability to our lives (1974: 11).

5. One need not wait long before things change in Unit 110. As this chapter was being revised, the *Pageville Press* informed its readers that after two years in office Burt Hanson had accepted a new job in a suburban district three times larger than Unit 110. He made several interesting comments in his final newspaper interview:

There's always something new [in Unit 110]. That's the thing that fires you up. . . . It's a hard job but it's fun. . . . Overall, the friction between communities is easing. . . . The individual communities feel very strongly about their schools and are very committed to the community school concept. . . . A superintendent, a staff, a school board, and citizens will eventually have to commit themselves to renovating, remodeling, and perhaps regrouping the district's five community elementary schools or abandoning them altogether for a completely centralized district. [September 30, 1979]

6. In the spring of 1980, as if to show that they had truly laid their case to rest, the KCC gave eighty dollars to the Killmer Parent-Teacher Organization and their remaining one thousand dollars to the Killmer park fund.

References

Aldrich, E. K. 1974. "Some Dynamics of Anticipatory Grief." In *Anticipatory Grief,* edited by Bernard Schoenberg et al. New York: Columbia University Press.

Alford, Robert R. 1960. "School District Reorganization and Community Integration," *Harvard Education Review* 30:350–71.

Arkin, A. M. 1974. "Notes on Anticipatory Grief." In *Anticipatory Grief,* edited by Bernard Schoenberg et al. New York: Columbia University Press.

Barker, Roger G., and Gump, Paul V. 1964. *Big School, Small School: High School Size and Student Behavior.* Stanford: Stanford University Press.

Bidwell, Charles E. 1965. "The School as a Formal Organization." In *Handbook of Organizations,* edited by J. G. March. Chicago: Rand McNally.

Boorstin, Daniel J. 1974. *The Americans: The Democratic Experience.* New York: Vintage Books.

Busch, Peter A. 1974. *Legitimacy and Ethnicity: A Case Study of Singapore.* Lexington, Mass.: Lexington Books.

Deising, Paul. 1962. *Reason in Society.* Urbana, Ill.: University of Illinois Press.

Fitzwater, C. O. 1953. *Educational Change in Reorganized School Districts.* Washington, D.C.: U.S. Government Printing Office.

Frost, Robert. 1946. "Mending Wall." In *The Poems of Robert Frost.* New York: The Modern Library.

Gehlen, F. L. 1969. *The Political Aspects of Small Towns and Rural Schools.* Las Cruces, N.M.: ERIC Clearinghouse on Rural Education and Rural Schools.

Good, Carter V. 1951. "The Terminology of District Organization."
    Phi Delta Kappan 32:344–45.
Henderson, Ronald, and Gomez, J. J. 1975. "The Consolidation of
    Rural Schools: Reasons, Results, and Implications—A Prelimi-
    nary Investigation." Paper presented at the annual meeting of the
    Rural Sociological Society, San Francisco.
Hirschman, A. O. 1970. *Exit, Voice, and Loyalty.* Cambridge, Mass.:
    Harvard University Press.
Jonassen, C. T. 1968. *Community Conflict in School District Reor-
    ganization,* Oslo: Universitetsforlaget.
Kraybill, Donald B. 1977. *Ethnic Education: The Impact of Men-
    nonite Schooling.* San Francisco: R and E Research Associates.
Kriesberg, Louis. 1973. *The Sociology of Social Conflicts.* Englewood
    Cliffs, N.J.: Prentice-Hall, Inc.
Marris, Peter. 1974. *Loss and Change.* London: Routledge and Kegan
    Paul.
Peshkin, Alan. 1978. *Growing Up American: Schooling and the Sur-
    vival of Community.* Chicago: University of Chicago Press.
Peters, R. S. 1965. "Education as Imitation." In *Philosophical Anal-
    ysis and Education,* edited by R. D. Archanbault. London: Rout-
    ledge and Kegan Paul.
Selznick, Philip. 1957. *Leadership in Administration.* Evanston, Ill.:
    Row, Peterson and Co.
Sher, Jonathon P., ed. 1977. *Education in Rural America: A Reas-
    sessment of Conventional Wisdom.* Boulder, Co.: Westview
    Press.
Spender, Stephen. 1979. "Civilization vs. Culture," a review of *The
    Dying Gaul* by David Jones (Salem, Mass.: Faber and Faber,
    1979). In *The New York Times Book Review* 9:26–27.
State of Illinois. 1945. *Manual for County School Survey Committees.*
    Springfield, Ill.: Superintendent of Public Instruction.
———. 1969. *The School Code of Illinois.* Springfield, Ill.
Strauss, Anselm. 1969. *Mirrors and Masks: The Search for Identity.*
    The Sociology Press.
Sumption, Merle, and Beem, Harlan D. 1947. *A Guide to School
    Reorganization in Illinois,* Champaign, Ill.: Bureau of Educa-
    tional Research.
Sumption, Merle and Engstrom, Yvonne. 1966. *School-Community
    Relations: A New Approach.* New York: McGraw-Hill.
United States Bureau of the Census. 1920–1970. *U.S. Census of Pop-
    ulation.* Washington, D.C.: U.S. Government Printing Office.
Webster's Third International Dictionary. 1968. Springfield, Mass.: G.
    and C. Merriam Co.

Index